"In *Confessions of a Wonder Woman Wannabe*, Jenny Sulpizio cuts through the drama of motherhood with a breath of fresh air. Her words are sugar to the soul of every modern-day mother on a quest to save her sanity while raising loving, God-centered children. With heart and humor, Sulpizio freely shares practical wisdom while readily admitting her need for earplugs, chocolate, and a heavy dose of grace. In 'waving the white flag' she reminds us that God didn't create Wonder Woman, our culture did. Yet she defies Wonder Woman by charging us to put our tiaras high on our heads and take our rightful position as daughters of the King. This book feels like an 'ah ha' conversation with a best friend."

—**Susan DiMickele**, author of *Working Women of the Bible* and *Chasing Superwoman*

"Jenny's book has helped take some of the mystery out of motherhood. I love how practical her advice is, down to effectively packing a car for 'emergencies.' She is honest about her struggles, making me feel better about mine. And her humor made me laugh out loud because I can relate to her stories. This is a perfect 'handbook' for new moms and seasoned ones alike. Regardless of what season of mothering you're in, this book is a must-have."

—**Carey Scott**, speaker, author, life coach

"I will never forget the day I left the hospital after giving birth to my first child. Panic struck as the thought went through my mind, 'They're letting me take this baby home with me!? I have no idea what to do once I get there!' Like most parents-to-be, new parents, and even experienced parents, I wanted to be the perfect mother to this precious bundle of joy that had entered into my world. Looking back on that moment, I can imagine the hope and confidence I would have gained had someone handed me a copy of this book! Jenny Lee Sulpizio gets what we as moms go through in our quest to be the best mom we can be; and she also gets the angst we feel when we fall short of our own ideals. You're going to love this book, moms! (And while you're at it, grab a copy for a friend! She'll thank you!)"

—**Shelley Hendrix,** author of *Why Can't We Just Get Along?*; founder of Church 4 Chicks

"As I read *Confessions of a Wonder Woman Wannabe,* I found myself thinking 'Me, too!' and 'Ah-HA!' on every page. I'm not the only mom who struggles valiantly (and vainly!) with gettin' to the church on time? *Whew!* I can pull out my dust-covered Crock Pot (or whatever it is) and learn how to use it? *Who knew!* There's a secret to keeping socks mated for life? *Finally!* I feel like I gained a new BFF and a practical parenting resource at the same time (and there's nothing this Wannabe loves more than a 2-for-1 deal!)."

—**Cheri Gregory**, co-author of *The Good Girl's Guide to Breaking Bad Rules*

"This book is a must read for any mom who has ever felt like she needed to be more than she already is. So I suppose it's a must read for ALL MOMS. In *Confessions of a Wonder Woman Wannabe,* Jenny Lee Sulpizio lets moms off the hook of striving to be perfect. With warm wit and vulnerability, Jenny gently dispels the myth of Super Mom while offering practical advice and spiritual encouragement for moms in the trenches."

—**Jessica Wolstenholm**, co-founder of graceformoms.com; co-author of *The Pregnancy Companion* and *The Baby Companion*

"*Confessions of a Wonder Woman Wannabe* by Jenny Lee Sulpizio is a gem of a book, useful for any mom who has ever felt overwhelmed and under-prepared for the tricky business of raising kids. Full of useful tips about facing and conquering the day-to-day life of a mom, and combined with gut-busting laughter and genuine encouragement—this book is a must for moms everywhere. Hooray for *Confessions of a Wonder Woman Wannabe*!"

—**Gillian Marchenko**, Christian, wife, mother, writer, speaker, www.gillianmarchenko.com

"Jenny Lee Sulpizio gives moms permission to let go of the *Wonder Woman Wannabe* within and instead embrace God's supernatural power in their lives. Filled with humor and practical advice, by the time you read the last page, you'll be inspired to be the mom you were created to be and wish more than once that you could hang out with Jenny a little longer."

—**Joanne Kraft**, author of *Just Too Busy—Taking Your Family on a Radical Sabbatical*

"It happens to all of us—we get this notion that motherhood is blissful and then reality sets in. Suddenly it's dirty diapers, up-all-nighters, and turning the minivan into a swagger wagon. This laugh-out-loud-funny resource tackles high expectations and gives moms the power to be Wonder Moms, with Jenny as your guide, giving you the how-tos in situations from stocking the minivan to reclaiming your identity as a woman. It›s a must have in any mom's library."

—**Heather Riggleman** is an over-caffeinated mom to three and the author of *Mama Needs a Time Out*, heatherriggleman.com

"Jenny Sulpizio is an author whose words go down easy. Her style is witty yet very informative. Even though the book lets us know we shouldn't attempt to be Wonder Woman, Sulpizio has some wonderful ideas for making motherhood easier, thus making us feel like Wonder Woman. This is a lighthearted yet helpful book."

—**Lucille Zimmerman**, Licensed Professional Counselor, Littleton, Colorado; affiliate faculty professor, Colorado Christian University; author of *Renewed: Finding Your Inner Happy in an Overwhelmed World*

"It gives me great pleasure to know that at least one other mom looked at her precious newborn baby just minutes after he or she was born and thought to herself, 'I have no clue what to do with this thing!' Isn't it so freeing to find out you're not the only one? If there's anything you can expect from *Confessions of a Wonder Woman Wannabe*, it's these two things: to know down in your knower you're not walking the motherhood road alone, and to laugh until you cry. Jenny Sulpizio is a master at communicating powerful truths with a zinging wit that makes us mamas feel like maybe we're normal after all."

—**Brooke McGlothlin**, co-founder of The MOB Society (FOR moms of boys, BY moms of boys) and co-author of *Hope for the Weary Mom: Where God Meets You in Your Mess*

# Confessions of a WONDER WOMAN WANNABE

# Confessions of a WONDER WOMAN WANNABE

ON A MISSION TO SAVE SANITY, ONE MOM AT A TIME!

JENNY LEE SULPIZIO

LEAFWOOD PUBLISHERS

**CONFESSIONS OF A WONDER WOMAN WANNABE**

*On a Mission to Save Sanity, One Mom at a Time*

LEAFWOOD
PUBLISHERS



ISBN 978-0-89112-392-7
LCCN 2013020751

Printed in the United States of America



Printed in association with The Seymour Agency, 475 Miner Street Road, Canton, New York 13617

---

LIBRARY OF CONGRESS CATALOGING-IN-PUBLICATION DATA
Sulpizio, Jenny Lee.
Confessions of a wonder woman wannabe : on a mission to save sanity, one mom at a time : / Jenny Lee Sulpizio.
pages cm
ISBN 978-0-89112-392-7
1. Motherhood--Religious aspects--Christianity. 2. Mothers--Religious life. I. Title.
BV4529.18.S85 2013
248.8'431--dc23

2013020751

---

Cover design by Marc Whitaker
Interior text design by Sandy Armstrong

Leafwood Publishers is an imprint of
Abilene Christian University Press
1626 Campus Court
Abilene, Texas 79601

1-877-816-4455
www.leafwoodpublishers.com

13 14 15 16 17 18 / 7 6 5 4 3 2 1

*I can do everything through him*
*who gives me strength.*

**—Philippians 4:13**

For my real life superheroes: my family.

*You are my blessings from above. Thank you for your support, love, and willingness to put up with me (not to mention that alter ego of mine) . . . to the moon and back. XOXO!*

# CONTENTS

## SECTION III: THE WONDER WOMAN WANNABE RECLAIMS HER IDENTITY (WELL . . . SORT OF)

# ACKNOWLEDGMENTS

On this crazy ride to publication, I must first thank God for the journey He's taking me on, and for the wisdom to trust Him no matter where it may lead (Jer. 29:11).

I absolutely must thank my agent, Mary Sue Seymour, and all of the fabulously talented and supportive authors that make up The Seymour Agency. I am blessed to be part of such a fantastic group!

A whole lot of gratitude must be extended to Leafwood Publishers and their decision to take a chance on little-old me. Thank you to my editor, Robyn Burwell, as well as Gary Myers, Ryan Self, Duane Anderson, Philip Dosa, and Seth Shaver, who've made my path to publication a lot easier (and oh-so-enjoyable).

I am humbled by the extended network of Christian authors and their willingness to support and care for a newbie to the group. Thank you Annette Irby, Erin MacPherson, Susan DiMickele, Laura Sabin Cabanillas, Brooke McGlothlin, Suzie Eller, The MOB Society, Moms Together, and the list goes on and on.

For my husband and the adventure we're on together. Thank you for your support, love, and understanding . . . and for just being you. I love you.

A special thanks to my mom and dad who have always stood by my side and supported each endeavor I've undertaken (no matter how many there have been). I love you both so very much. Thank you to my mother-in-law, Sue, who's been busy scouting book signing venues ever since I initially signed on to write this guide. It's appreciated more than you know. XOXO

For my best friends, Kari Bhana and Lori Phillips—I love you girls. Thank you for your encouraging words, love, and amazing friendship all these years . . . and now that this book's been published, hopefully we can hang out once in a while!

Last, but never least, to my three amazing children who've not only provided me with plenty of material to write this book, but many more to come. I'm so blessed to be your mommy and you're loved more than you'll ever know.

For every mother . . . everywhere.

# PREFACE

My Fellow Mamas,

After picking up this book, I know what you might be thinking at this point: Why is a full-grown, Christian woman with tons of responsibilities, a husband, and three kiddos of her own confessing her innermost desire to channel a fictitious superheroine, of all things? I mean, what is it about Wonder Woman that she's so desperately trying to emulate and why?

Well, if you're anything like me, the answer is simple.

You see, as a mommy in the midst of motherhood, I don't necessarily meet the requirements society has set in place for me. Last time I checked, I'm no June Cleaver, nor do I even remotely resemble the likes of Martha Stewart. And as you might have already guessed, I'm certainly no Wonder Woman, either. I'm just your typical, imperfect mama who tends to burn cookies (way too often), and bake casseroles that, at times, mimic the food I feed my dog. I'm also a gal who fails miserably when it comes to understanding the purpose of a needle and thread (no, really!), gets traffic tickets (way too often), watches too much reality television, and desperately desires alone time, all of the time. For me (and maybe for you, too), modern-day motherhood has become this uncomfortable breeding ground for multitasking madness, overwhelming struggles, and unhealthy competition . . . which begs all of us moms to truthfully answer the real question here: Who wouldn't want to be perfect? Who wouldn't want to be Wonder Woman?

Well friends, this book was written with you in mind, because, let's face it, there are too many mamas out there just like us—harassed by the stigmas associated with motherhood and by that Wonder Woman complex we're choosing to embrace. As a collective group, most of us find ourselves desperately searching for answers on how to do this parenting gig correctly and efficiently, while hoping to produce happy, spiritually sound kiddos in the process. We seek assistance through self-help books, television programs, the Internet, and magazine articles. We confide in other moms willing to share their stories, tips, and expertise on how to play this part the best way possible. We pray for our children at what seems like every moment of every day. But we're still stuck, still needing help, and still struggling.

In essence, we are the Wonder Woman Wannabes, and this is our plight.

But take heed, precious mamas—it doesn't have to be this way. Even though we may not possess a lasso of truth or have bullet-proof wristbands in our arsenal, moms like us are equipped with some pretty awesome superpowers of our own . . . and it's about time we start realizing it.

Remember, girls: God didn't create Wonder Woman; our culture did. Our God made us imperfect for a reason. He knew we would endure trials and tribulations. But just as He promised that this life wouldn't be easy, He also gave us the hope that it would all be worth it.

So, what do you say Wannabes? Let's crack open this book and get started. Let's take on motherhood, and all of its mayhem, together.

*"I have told you these things, so that in me you may have peace. In this world you will have trouble. But take heart! I have overcome the world."*

**—John 16:33**

# INTRODUCTION

WILL THE REAL WONDER WOMAN PLEASE STAND UP?

I'll confess: it all started at the tender age of five.

There I stood, hands perched upon my hips, my trusty lasso in tow, donning one mean pair of retro-seventies, ultra-hip, and all-powerful Wonder Woman Underoos®. The final touch? None other than a golden tiara placed regally upon my head. That's right. I was capable of anything and everything that your average five-year-old could handle. I was indestructible. Cool. Strong. Practically perfect. I *was* Wonder Woman.

Or at least I *thought* I was.

Five-year-olds don't necessarily have a grip on reality.

Thirty-five-year-olds? Most of us *do. Sigh.*

However, it wasn't until the ripe old age of ten came around, and those Underoos had long been outgrown, that it became apparent Wonder Woman was nothing more than make-believe. A myth. An imaginary icon, if you will. Kind of like Santa Claus, but without the presents and annual trips to the mall. And if this wasn't bad enough, it also turned out that leaping tall buildings, lassoing others into telling the truth, and turning around in a circle faster than the speed of light in order to change into one's superhero outfit was not only unrealistic but pretty nauseating as well. Yes, as painful as it was to admit, my superhero role model was nothing more than than a fictitious character. She had no *real* superpowers to speak of, and other than her fabulous and oh-so-fashionable attire, she appeared to be nothing more than just an ordinary woman with no "wonder" attached to her.

So at the even riper age of thirty-five, why have I been trying to channel her for so long? Why have I put so much pressure on myself in order to be everything and more to my family when *Lord knows* I'm not perfect (nor anywhere close)? Maybe it's the fact that she's perceived as being all-powerful, smart, beautiful, and capable of handling anything thrown her way, all while rocking a wicked pair of stiletto boots. Or, maybe it's the fact that everything in her world appears unblemished, ideal, and that she is, in essence, perfect.

As I just mentioned, I'm nowhere near perfect. In fact, I'm just a normal, Christian gal trying to raise her kids in a big, scary world. I'm a regular old mom, aren't I? Or am I something more?

You might be wondering the same thing.

Well, if you ask me, there's nothing *regular* about being a mom. Rather, there's something wondrous about it. You see, you may not only be a mother, but a wife, domestic engineer, bug slayer, party-planner guru, nurturer, nurse, chauffer, cheerleader, drill sergeant, prayer warrior, disciplinarian, craft and activity supervisor, and a slew of other jobs that we ladies keep tucked nice and tidy under those belts of our "Mom jeans." We also wipe boogers, clean bottoms, make dinner, run errands, and attempt to continually do it all on a daily basis, despite the fact that we are only human. Guess what, girls? It sounds like we might be the ones with the real superpowers after all.

But no matter how strong or how independent we ladies might deem ourselves to be, every Wonder Woman Wannabe needs their sanity shielded at all costs. Plain and simple, Supermoms need some super help. We need advice. We need prayer. And we may be in need of an instruction manual (in addition to the Bible that is) to help guide us on this journey known as motherhood. Let me just say that assistance has arrived and you, my friend, are about to get some much-needed relief from someone who can relate to everything you're going through (and then some). Yes, ladies—it's time to save your sanity, ignore your need for perfection, and absorb the fun-filled, helpful advice this book was written to provide you with.

These are the confessions of a Wonder Woman Wannabe.

# SECTION I

# THE WONDER WOMAN WANNABE TACKLES MOTHERHOOD

# 1

# YOU'RE A MOM . . . NOW WHAT?

*"There is no way to be a perfect mother,*
*and a million ways to be a good one."*

**—Jill Churchill**

And there she lay. After forty-one-and-a-half weeks of pregnancy, and eighteen long, and rather painful—make that excruciating—hours of labor, my daughter had officially arrived. And it was at that point that I realized . . . I had absolutely no clue what I was supposed to do with her. Other than admiring that sweet, beautiful miracle, wrapped like a little burrito in her swaddling blanket and asleep in my arms, I was frighteningly devoid of my maternal instincts and just waiting for something (anything!), to kick in.

"Excuse me," I said as I spoke into the hospital room intercom, attempting to grab the attention of one of the attending nurses. "I'm ready for my infant to be taken to the nursery now."

There was silence on the other end.

"Hello?" I said again, maniacally pressing the button in an effort to get some attention. "Can anyone hear me? I'm pretty tired and need some assistance with getting my daughter settled for the night."

It was at that point that I could have sworn I heard cackling in the background as the nurse dispatch seemingly collected herself, paused for a moment, and then stated, "Um, we don't have a nursery, sweetie," trying hard to hold back laughter. "That baby girl of yours is bunking with you tonight . . . and every night from here on out."

Puzzled by her response and quite certain she had made a mistake, I looked at my husband in disbelief. With my hormones raging and tears welling up in my bloodshot eyes, I glanced down at my beautiful baby girl and pathetically yelped, "Help me!"

As a new mom, my mind was anxious with inexperience, as question after question on how I should mother this infant kept popping into my head: *Why was this baby sleeping so long? What should I do with her if she wakes up? What happens when she has a dirty diaper? Should I ring the nurse to come and change her? In fact, where was the nurse most of the time and why wasn't she taking care of this baby for me? Wait, why was my hospital gown all wet? Were my breasts leaking? Dear God, what was going on with my body?*

And then the ultimate in negative thinking infiltrated my brain: *Maybe I just wasn't cut out for this motherhood gig after all. I mean maybe, just maybe, if I could bribe that delivery nurse to come home with me and agree to be my live-in nanny, this might all work out. After all, she did appear to have a sense of humor and definitely seemed like she'd be good with kids.*

As it turns out, this "rational" plan of attack I concocted probably wasn't going to be the best long-term solution after all, especially since bribery tends to work best when you actually have money. But hey, I was a new mommy and feeling a bit overwhelmed by the helplessness and sleep deprivation I was experiencing since that sweet blessing had arrived safely in my arms. Sure, I had been forewarned of the challenges that these first few days might present, but in all honesty, I didn't believe they would happen to me. You see, prior to becoming a mom, I'd read book after book on how to be a great mother, how to avoid being a bad one, and everything in between. I felt prepared, confident, and ready to defy those "supposed" issues that most new mommies face: Raging hormones? Please, mine would be even-keel. Colicky baby? *Pshaw!* Had to be a myth. Complete and total exhaustion to the point where one's eyelids needed to be pried open with toothpicks? Sounded like complete nonsense to me.

Yep, upon becoming a mother, it appeared that not only was I slightly delusional as to the expectations I had for myself, but it also seemed that I was suffering from a bit of naivety, a hint of denial, and was under the trance of one serious perfectionist complex already. Unbeknownst to me, my Wonder Woman Wannabe alter-ego (complete with imbalanced hormones) was taking up residence within, and the Supermom Syndrome was well underway.

"I think you just need to breathe," my husband said.

"Breathe?" I asked quizzically, as if he were speaking a foreign language or something.

"Yeah, as in inhale, exhale, and repeat."

"Oh, yeah . . . right," I said. "B-R-E-A-T-H-E. Maybe I should try that."

If only those superpowers would kick in already.

> *"There will be so many times you feel like you've failed.*
> *But in the eyes, heart and mind of your child*
> *you are Super Mom."*
>
> **—Stephanie Precourt**

## STRUGGLING TO BECOME "SUPER"

Remembering those first few months of motherhood kind of makes me cringe. Now, please don't take my words the wrong way—I was enamored of that beautiful baby I had been given, and was quite aware of how blessed I was. What I struggled with were the changes that came with being a new mom: figuring out which of my baby's cries meant what, how the whole issue of feeding was supposed to take place, and understanding how to operate (and fully function) on three hours of sleep. In fact, I think I'm still struggling with that one.

Adjustments such as these, well, let's just say they come along with the territory . . . and they're all part of being a new mom. Unfortunately for me, though, I didn't get the memo. Instead, my induction into this "maternal sorority" wasn't the smooth transition I had originally hoped for, and those early days spent in "the motherhood" transpired a bit differently than the visions I had spent years conjuring up in my head. You see, initially, I had expectations of a well-orchestrated daily schedule comprised of pure baby bliss: maybe routine trips to the gym, long showers, and a much-needed nap or two (or three) each day. Throw in the gourmet meals I was going to whip up for my husband each night, and the spotless house I was going to regularly maintain, and I was convinced of my destiny to redefine the "super" in Supermom . . . and channel my inner Wonder Woman in the process, I might add.

I'm sure you can guess what happened instead.

The truth of the matter was this: after becoming a mom, my world consisted of a constant struggle to maintain balance in my life. It was evident that all of those ambitious ideas I once possessed were totally ridiculous on my part, and the reality of my situation was that I hardly ever worked out, cooked macaroni and cheese out of the box, a lot, and detested the mere thought of cleaning my own home. I was run-down, tired, and in need of assistance. My clothes didn't fit, my hair was a mess, and that unblemished, outward facade I once possessed was long gone. I was forced into accepting the fact that my life on this roller coaster ride of motherhood was going to require every ounce of energy I could muster, a whole lot of help from up above, and maybe a serious caffeine addiction, as well.

But wait. Wasn't this "ride" supposed to be amazing?

Amazing? Yes! Perfect? No.

Were doubts, questions, and moments of pure pandemonium going to surface?

Absolutely.

Would I become the type of mother who'd pray incessantly, all the while enduring bouts of temporary insanity, a jolted confidence, and the severe testing of my patience along the way?

Odds were, likely.

Was I going to mess up from time to time, struggle with imperfection a lot, and question my parenting abilities just as often?

All signs would point to "yes."

But who told me I needed to be perfect? And who said that my best wasn't going to be good enough? It certainly wasn't God. Nope, that person was me. I was a new mom struggling to become "super" . . . and I was losing the battle, big time.

## SO, NOW WHAT?

Throughout this journey, I've learned a thing or two, or five hundred, about parenting my clan of three. At this point in my tenure, I'm finally understanding what works, what doesn't, and what will single-handedly drive me to the brink of insanity without hopes of ever returning. Hey, there's no denying that motherhood is a blessing and those children of ours are without question miracles, but that doesn't mean raising them is easy, now does it?

In fact, ever since birthing my beautiful brood, I've morphed into a woman that, at times, I hardly recognize. I don't say this to scare you of course, but I must confess that my mind has become pretty scattered (okay—make that seriously spacey). That useless '80s music trivia I once prided myself on knowing is now a thing of the past. Dates, names, faces, and childhood memories have seemingly retreated to an unknown destination within my brain, and I'm lucky if I leave the house each morning without sporting my ensemble inside out, upside down, or displaying unsightly deodorant stains. This mom (yep, me) has been found in public on more than one occasion donning two different shoes, a bra gone AWOL, and hair that would never be categorized as cute. Those days of carrying on an adult conversation (you know—using words other than "caca" and "binky") are long gone, and instead of putting my college degrees to use, I simply have them hanging on the wall to help remind me that I even went to college at all.

*"Enjoy every single moment. The good, the bad, the beautiful, the ugly, the inspiring, the not-so-glamorous moments. And thank God through it all."*

**—Meghan Matt**

So, now what?

Girls, I think most of us can agree that we possess the desire to become more prepared, better organized, less frazzled mothers. I myself spend a sizeable amount of time praying for more patience, less frustration, and for God to mold me into the type of mom I so desperately want to become—perhaps one who's even a little less absent-minded at times. Hey, I don't deny that, on occasion, I've even prayed for God to grant me some sort of superpowers, as well. Maybe not bionic strength or X-ray vision, but perhaps an extra arm or two for multitasking purposes, the ability to turn back time after a not-so-great mommy meltdown, the option to clone myself so I can be in ten different places at once, or simply the power to be everything to everyone during every moment of every day (without collapsing in utter exhaustion).

You, too, might be in search of easier ways to accomplish specific tasks and complete those unending errands. And you might also be a mom who finds herself stuck in a routine that she just can't work her way out of. Like you, I wanted to be more structured. I wanted to be more prepared. I wanted less stress in my life and more time for those memorable mommy moments I was craving with my young'uns.

I wanted all of these things and more, but didn't know where to start or how to begin decoding the mystery of motherhood.

After all, there isn't a cheat sheet, nor are there crib notes we can reference. The manual I was in desperate need of to help me figure out how to do this role of mine—broken down by age and gender, and inclusive of all those unexpected surprises that would most certainly pop up on this journey—just didn't exist. But through my experience, and inexperience, I began to glean some valuable insight into this role. I found that the unexpected should be expected. I finally began to understand and appreciate what the concept of true patience really meant, and that being present day in and day out in the lives of my children, and loving them with my whole heart, was the most important thing I could do for them. I learned all of these things and more through ups and downs, highs and lows (a nervous breakdown or two . . . kidding, of course), and ultimately, through divine intervention.

But enough chit-chat already, right? Let's get started by providing you with the information you're looking for. After all, this guide is in your hands in order to give you the tips you'll need to make your life easier. And it's been written to give you the practical advice you're searching for, with the Christian foundation we all need.

## THE THREE BASIC RULES OF MOTHERHOOD

So, what are the three basic rules of motherhood that every Wonder Woman Wannabe should know?

I'm so glad you asked.

### *1. Expect the unexpected.*

I'll be honest in stating that I haven't always been a prepared mom. In fact, there have been plenty of times where I have jumped in the car, kids in tow, only to forget some pretty important necessities. You know—items that no mother should be without? We're talking diapers, wipes, jackets (in the dead of winter), my cell phone, shoes—of all things, how does one forget shoes?—and the list goes on and on. You name it and I have forgotten it, because I have failed to take the necessary steps in preparing myself in advance.

It's in those times that I seriously think my mommy card should be revoked.

But in order to stave off stress and avoid embarrassment, moms need to be uber-organized. If you haven't heard this before, I'm telling you now: preparation is key when it comes to being a mom. Whether it be packing your kiddo's diaper bag the night before in order to avoid the last-minute, early-morning scuffle or simply making a list to remind yourself of your child's necessities, being prepared is vital to your sanity and overall well-being. Want to make sure you're ready for when the unexpected happens to you? How about trying these tips on for size?

**Make a list:** Now, I'm a Capricorn by birth, which means that I am a maker of all things list-like. Is that even a word? No, seriously, if there's a list to be made for any reason at all, I'm the gal making one. And my advice to you would be to do the same. Keep a journal, a daily planner, use apps on your cell phone, or whatever else will help you stay on task and be more organized. Believe me—you'll be glad you did!

**Maintain a schedule:** I absolutely *must* keep track of my appointments, including any event I'm scheduled to make some sort of appearance at, or they become completely lost in the recesses of my brain. I'm a mom, I've had kids, and that means my memory is shot (we've been over this before, right?). It's a given. But part of being prepared for day-to-day endeavors is knowing where you have to be, at what time, and for how long. This requires a bit of planning and some organization. Use your cell phone calendar to keep on task, or establish a wall calendar at home so your spouse, kids, and anybody else interested in your activities can be "in the know." Keeping an up-to-date schedule is a huge sanity saver, girls.

**Get help:** I am a mom of three. I'll let you do the math here, but since there is only one of me and three of them, this would indicate that I am severely outnumbered when it comes to my mothering duties. I need help. In fact, I need a lot of help. Confessing this doesn't make me weak, nor does it make me less of a mom . . . it simply makes me aware of the fact that I need assistance (and that I should never be too proud to ask for it). Do yourselves a favor, moms, and employ neighbors, friends, in-laws, parents, or whoever else can help you as often as possible. Help is needed . . . and usually just a phone call away.

### *2. A little patience, please.*

Who else out there finds themselves quick-tempered and easily frustrated? I've got both of my hands held high on this question and will be the first to admit that part of the problem with me resides in the fact that I no longer think like a kid. I think like an adult instead, and expect my kids to think (and act) the same way that I do.

But as Mark Merrill once stated, "Patience is choosing to control your emotions rather than letting your emotions control you."

Hey, our kids are going to make mistakes. They're human. At times, they're going to do things that make absolutely no sense at all, in this lifetime or any other. They're going to act out, behave poorly, throw tantrums, and embarrass the heck out of us, but guess what? They're kids, and the whole concept of good behavior just so happens to be a learned one. It's how we respond to those crazy situations that make all the difference. Yelling and screaming won't get you anywhere (believe me, I've tried), but controlling your tongue, using reason instead, and implementing the use of prayer most definitely will. When your patience is all but gone, try a few of these tips to help you keep your cool.

**Count to ten . . . or eighty:** For me, ten seconds won't cut it. In order to still my temper and reach that happy place (within) once again, I shoot for eighty seconds instead. Take some deep, calming breaths and try to breathe your way through the frustration. Remember those Lamaze breathing methods you once used to deliver your now tantrum-throwing toddler? Time to brush off those birthing manuals and bust out those techniques all over again. Breathe away that frustration and keep your cool when tempers threaten to rage. It's worth a try, right?

**Pray:** In fact, pray like you've never prayed before. I find it helpful to sound off in the middle of my frustration: "Lord, help me now, because (enter child's name here) is trying my patience. I need you to let him know that I can't take it anymore. Will you please help (said child's name) to become a sweet, loving, and respectful kid? You know, the kind of gentleman (or young lady) you call him to be? Lord, hear my prayer. Amen."

Hey, God knows when you're about to flip your lid, and He's aware of how trying His little creations can be. So, seek Him out for help anytime you're being tested and your sanity is in question. Better yet, ask God for help first and go to Him always . . . and often.

**Keep calm and carry on:** I feel like this phrase was written especially for me. Keep this saying close to your heart, fresh on your mind, and maybe plaster it somewhere in your home as a reminder when times get tough—because frustration is inevitable when you're a mommy, which means we had better find ways to deal with it appropriately. Amen? Keep calm girls . . . breathe, pray, relax, repeat.

### *3. Be there or be square*

Life can get pretty crazy at times—as in the out-of-control, cuckoo type of crazy. Time speeds by much too quickly. I often find myself anxiously wondering how in the heck my children grew to their current ages and fretting over how soon their sweet childhoods will be but memories (ones I *hope* I'll be able to remember, that is). It's downright scary. All those efforts to freeze time have failed miserably. But even if we mamas can't stop the clock, we do possess the power to make the most of the time we have by enjoying our children purposely, willfully, with our whole hearts, and with 100 percent of our attention. Being present means being deliberate in everything we do with our kiddos. It means refusing to allow the mindless, monotonous jobs of motherhood—cooking, cleaning, laundering, and so on—to consume us. Instead, we need to focus on the larger picture ahead by not getting wrapped up in the small, meaningless stuff. Confused? Let me clarify:

**Together time:** Set aside a period each day to spend intentional time with your kids. Read together before bed, watch a favorite family television show, talk about the day's events, play a board game, or better yet, spend some much-needed time in Scripture. No matter what you do, make these designated moments of the day routine for your child. You know, a portion of the day they can count on and look forward to spending with *you*.

**Listen up:** As a mom, my mind just happens to always be in motion. Whether it's trying to remember if I turned the Crock-Pot on this morning or whether I failed to turn the curling iron off, my brain is never at rest. Come to find out, my children are the same way. But rather than keeping their thoughts to themselves, they'd much rather express them . . . every single one of them, out loud and all of the time. As moms, we need to listen to our kiddos. We need to turn off our minds and turn on our ears. It doesn't matter if our kids don't make sense or if the vocabulary they're using doesn't exactly equate to English. They feel happy, secure, and safe enough to share with us all that's going on in that brain of theirs, and they're begging for a captive audience. So, let's make a concerted effort to place our thoughts on hold as we intentionally listen to what their young minds have to say. Because chances are, if we don't pay attention now, they won't give us the time of day later.

**Limit technology:** Cell phones, computers, tablets, and other technological devices that have made their way into our lives are also the instruments currently stripping us from valuable time with our families and loved ones. I'm just as guilty as anyone else of letting these electronic contraptions invade my life. Try curbing your use of these devices, especially when at home, and tend to your social media needs well after they've gone to bed.

If only motherhood were this easy though, right? If only these simple practices mentioned above could be the answers to all of our questions and the solutions to all of our mommy dilemmas. But keep in mind: this is only Chapter One, girls. Hang on tight, have no fears, and keep on reading.

2

# ROLLIN' IN MY ~~5.0~~ MINIVAN

*"A suburban mother's role is to deliver children obstetrically once, and by car forever after."*

**—Peter De Vries**

I know what you're thinking . . . Wonder Woman, or any of the other Super Friends, wouldn't be caught dead in the likes of a minivan. And you know what? You're probably right. But it's no secret that as practical, twenty-first century moms, we certainly don't have access to invisible airplanes or any other superhuman mode of transportation. And let's be honest: those days of looking cool, trendy, and just plain modish in those cute four-seaters we once possessed are a distant memory. Today, we're in need of a "ride" that's functional, efficient, low maintenance, and gets great gas mileage. We need a car capable of hauling up to ten people at a time (not to mention all of their school supplies, sports gear, and electronic devices). This description doesn't exactly scream convertible, now does it? Rather, most of us moms have come to grips with the fact that in order to tow our precious cargo in the most efficient manner possible, we need to invest in the ultra-unhip and oh-so-unflattering station wagon of modern times. Gulp.

You guessed it—I'm talking about the minivan.

It seems like just yesterday I found myself at the car dealership—*me, of all people*—checking out the latest and greatest in boats on wheels. I, yes, *I!*, was interested in purchasing a minivan . . . an event I never thought could happen in my lifetime. Now, don't get me wrong. I'm not discounting the privilege afforded to me of being able to purchase such a car, but I just never pictured myself as a mom in a big, honkin' wagon. But there I was—recently sprung from my SUV after its transmission went on the fritz—test-driving the one vehicle I swore I would never, ever, acquire for myself. After all, a minivan meant the end to any ounce of "cool" I still possessed. And as a gal currently sporting her thirties, I was trying to hold on to any remaining shred of it I could. Let me tell you, I had spent years resisting—clawing, scratching, screaming, and fighting—this purchase, but it was apparent that I could do so no longer. With three children, one husband, two dogs and a schedule of activities that was slightly out of control, I reluctantly embraced the idea of becoming the newest soccer mom to hit the road in one of these machines.

I was about to become a minivan mama.

And how could I not? After sliding into the driver's seat, and opening my wedged-shut eyes and clenched fists, I became pleasantly surprised by the display laid out in front of me. The look of protest that had been disfiguring my face from the moment we stepped foot on to that car lot was instantly gone. And as my initial test-drive got under way, I began thinking that maybe, and I'm saying *maybe* here, this *thing* wasn't *so* bad after all. I mean, I had everything at my disposal in this ~~boat~~ car: lots of lights, gadgets, mirrors, and too many mommy options to count. I could fit a whole baseball team in the trunk alone if I wanted to, and the booming sound system that accompanied this "ride" had me instantly reverting back to the days when society considered me hip. In fact, it seemed only natural that I would crank up the base, roll down my child-proof safety windows, and dial that radio to the first '80s station I could find.

But I wasn't done yet.

After belting "Don't Stop Believing," from the top of my lungs—and embarrassing my husband, as only I am quite capable of doing—at the press of a button, I threw that driver's seat into full-tilt mode. And with my wrist cradling the steering wheel, my shades on, and my foot pressed firmly on the gas, revving the RPMs, I took to the streets and began to cruise . . . in a minivan of all things.

The look upon the car dealer's face as he sat next to me was one of utter surprise. He was shocked, perhaps traumatized, and unable to formulate words. His eyes were large and he appeared to be motionless—incapable of processing what was transpiring on this most unusual of test-drives. But, I was too busy reinventing the minivan to care about the humiliation I was causing this poor guy. Besides, he was about to make a sale on this converted minivan protester, so he had better attempt to make a decent co-pilot, and honorary Journey fan, *stat!*

It was at that point that I changed. I was no longer a skeptic. I looked forward to taking to the streets in this thing. I was giddy over the convenience this machine would bring to my life in my daily mommy endeavors. I was thankful that this ~~tank~~ car was a safe and effective means of toting my family to and fro. I was going to be the next newly clad minivan mama . . . and I was actually excited about it!

Wait, me?

Yes, *me*!

Never say never, girls.

## THE PRIDE'S IN MY RIDE

*"In my Swagger Wagon,*
*Yeah, the Swagger Wagon,*
*I got the pride in my ride."*

**—Toyota Sienna Minivan theme song**

Not all of us drive minivans, but as moms, one thing is for sure: we spend a lot, and I mean a lot, of time in our cars. It's our second home, of sorts, which means we need to stock that thing from front end to rear bumper in order to make sure we're ready for all the emergencies life, and our kids, will dish out on the road. From vomit bags to first aid kits, we need to be prepared, because as I've mentioned before (and will tend to do *ad nauseum* throughout this book), being prepared is crucial to reducing our stress and keeping this game of motherhood manageable.

So, what kinds of stuff do you need to keep on hand? How should you take care of your car? And better yet, what's *really* necessary to have for emergencies and the like? I've got your answers right here, girls, so make sure to equip your cars with the following:

### *The Trunk*

The trunk is definitely the one area of our vehicles where things tend to accumulate. I know this because the more room I have in my trunk, the more stuff tends to find its way back there. Yes, I have junk in my trunk . . . lots of it, in fact. The same holds true for the rest of my vehicle, as well. Broken toys, abandoned articles of clothing, and pieces of food that couldn't quite find the mouths of my children have all become senseless victims, and even casualties, in that automobile of mine. But rather than becoming a wasteland for old trinkets, half-eaten candy, and toddler underwear that may never see the light of day again, my minivan needs to be equipped with items that will help me stave off stress, keep me sane, and prevent any minor kiddo injury from becoming a major one along the way.

Plain and simple: as mommies, our trunks need to house an emergency preparedness kit . . . and a good one at that.

Now, at the store you can find some pretty great travel kits. They come complete with Band-Aids, burn cream, a vat of antibacterial ointment, and what seems to be a lifetime supply of gauze pads. These items are perfect when confronted with a minor burn or laceration, but I must conclude that we need (much) more than a bunch of bandages when it comes to keeping our cool within our cars. Amen? We need a customized collection of sanity-saving supplies that will address every sort of mommy emergency, as well. We need a "Cuckoo Prevention Kit" that will help us fend off the "crazies," maintain our calm, and assist us when facing any and every type of crisis on the road.

## *1. Cuckoo Prevention Kits: Emergency Must-Haves for Your Car*

CPKs can be broken down into two basic areas: (1) kiddie crisis combatives, and (2) sanity-saving mommy must-haves. Think of these kits as disaster preparedness for you, your children, and your car. Now, what you choose to place in your kit is completely up to you. If you have an infant, obviously you are going to need a lot more items than the list of suggestions I've compiled below. Remember, this is a collection to be developed for and by you, based on what your own individual family's needs may be.

### Kiddie Crises Combatives

**Vomit bags:** Next time you fly, forget the extra bags of peanuts and stock up on those vomit receptacles for your CPK, instead. You know, the ones located behind the instructions on how to use your seat as a flotation device? These containers can have many uses, depending on your needs, but are excellent for holding their contents (without spilling) and can be secured shut after use. *Ew!*

Don't fly that much? Throw a few gallon-sized plastic bags, that will close securely, in your kit and they'll work just as well. Whatever you do, have some sort of puke-catching device in your car. Maybe throw in a small can of deodorizing spray while you're at it, because that is one smell that is hard to rid your vehicle of and may just make you want to heave yourself.

**Water:** Safely store at least two extra bottles of purified drinking water in the trunk of your car. By stocking these in your trunk, and out of plain sight, your kiddos won't mistakenly use them for an afternoon beverage. But just to make sure, label and date them: "For Emergency Use Only." Hopefully, that will keep your children's hands off of them and help preserve them for their intended use.

**Snacks:** We all know how our children tend to get when there's a hunger inside of them, right? I have to admit that I'm the same way when my belly starts a rumblin'. In fact, it's reason enough to declare a national state of emergency in our little family. Ward off whining and any potential for a major breakdown by having non-perishable snacks on hand to help calm those manic munchies and prevent unwanted (and unecessary) trips to the drive-thru. Restock as needed.

**Change of clothes for each child:** This is *muy importante, chicas*! Make sure that you have a change of clothes (including socks, undies, and shoes) for each of your children. For whatever reason, kids are magnets for pee, poop, barf, mud, blood, or any other type of mystery fluid that can find a way onto those bodies of theirs. By being prepared with an extra set of clothes, stored in a re-sealable plastic bag and labeled with your child's name on it, you can breathe a huge sigh of relief the next time your child falls prey to a messy accident. *Phew!*

**Wipes:** Wipes can be used for practically anything and everything under the sun, so make sure to have plenty of them on hand for issues that should (or could) arise. Grab a small travel-size bag at the store and place it in your kit. You may also want to stock a few washcloths or possibly a roll of paper towels in order to handle the bigger spills. And as we all know, those definitely tend to happen.

**Diapers:** If you have young'uns who still require the use of diapers, then you need to place at least five or six of these in your emergency kit—this is in addition to what you currently have in your diaper bag. We all know blowouts can happen, depleting your supply to the point where emergency backup may need to be called in. Just make sure they are the right size for your baby's bum, and change out your stock as needed.

**Sunscreen:** Although I'm not *technically* considered to be an Albino, one thing is for certain: my skin burns the moment it's exposed to sun. Sunscreen is a definite must for me and my pasty brood. But you don't have to be a lighter shade of pale to understand how important sunscreen is for all skin types. Hey, it's a necessity no matter the season, so make sure to always have a can/bottle/tube accessible, and apply liberally to your children each and every day.

**Travel potty:** Pick up a collapsible, travel potty for those times when a bathroom is nowhere to be found, but the immediate need to empty one's bladder is. These are super handy to have, even if your kids are potty trained, because as we all know so well, nature tends to call at the most inopportune times. Invest in a travel potty and you'll be one happy camper, whether you're in the woods or in the parking lot at the mall. This is a must-have item.

**Hand sanitizer:** I own stock in this stuff. Let me rephrase that: I *should* own stock in this stuff. Pick-up a few travel-size bottles for your kit or maybe a large vat of this germ-eating goo for the inside of your car, and use generously.

**Medications:** These can be extremely important to have on hand, especially if your child suffers from allergic reactions or has another medical condition that may require immediate care. More than likely, these will be kept with you and not in your kit, but there are some meds like fever-reducer, acetamenophin, and the like that you would like to have just in case. Keep all medications child- and tamper-proof, updated, and stored in a *cool* place.

**Flashlights:** Make sure to have a small flashlight in your kit in case of an emergency at night . . . or if your kids just want to use it to tell ghost stories in your vehicle. Either way, keep one on hand and check its batteries often. These things definitely come in handy.

**Boredom busters:** To keep yourself sane on car trips, or even just quick runs to the store, have some activities and games on hand that are kiddie- and car-friendly (as in, won't make a mess). Think washable crayons, markers, pens, pencils, notepads, journals, coloring books, or anything else you can think of to curb kiddie chaos. Keep them stored nicely in a small, plastic container and make sure that all items used end up back in your kit and not on the floorboard of your car.

**Batteries:** Batteries are expensive, but so is losing your mind if you don't have them in your CPK. You'll need these guys for your flashlight and any other mobile, electronic device your children may or may not be currently addicted to. Hey, this is the age of technology, which means our kids have gadgets, and lots of them. Invest in some batteries, keep them in a cool, dry place in the trunk, and by all means, check to make sure you have the right sizes for the right devices. Just sayin!

### Seasonal Items

Now, if you live in areas where there are four fabulous seasons, and most of us do, you need to prepare and alter your kits accordingly by changing out some of your items. For instance, if it's twenty below outside and your child just threw-up all over herself, her baby sister, and the innocent by-stander—the dog lying in her lap—and the only items you've got in your CPK are befitting for the summertime, you've got a serious problem . . . not to mention a whole lot of mess to clean up. Depending on the time of year, you'll want to have some of these specific items stocked:

**De-Icer:** Being able to see through your windshield while driving in the snow is a definite bonus. Keep the right tools in your trunk in order to adjust to inclement weather, as well as prevent any type of minor emergency. If you live in an area where chains are needed in snowy weather, it's probably best to have them in your car. Snow can create major havoc, not to mention super unsafe driving conditions. Have all necessary items stored in your trunk so you're prepared to deal with poor weather conditions effectively. We're all about preventing emergencies, not creating them.

**Jackets:** These can be pretty bulky when it comes to storing them in our vehicles, but by using hangers and your mini-van's stellar clothes hook (located in the trunk), they'll be out of sight and out of your way. Or, if you have one of those cars with amazing secret storage under the seats, use those compartments to house the bulkier items that you'd rather not have taking up valuable space in the cabin of your car. And if you don't relate to either of the examples mentioned above, I would highly recommend investing in storage bags specifically meant for housing large items. You know, the ones in which all the air can be sucked out, causing the contents within to lay flat and take up very little room? Jackets, blankets, and other wintertime apparel may be a must for us during the winter season, but it doesn't mean they have to become space hogs in the process.

**Winter accessories:** Jackets aren't the only things needed when Jack Frost is hard at work. Gloves, hats, and socks are all items that have the irritating ability of constantly getting misplaced . . . and believe me when I tell you that searching for my son's long-lost Spiderman glove in the freezing cold is enough to send me over the edge, begging for some sanity. Try storing your kiddos' gloves, hats, and socks in individual, zippable plastic bags, instead. Label them with your children's names and sizes. By keeping these sets in your kit, you'll ensure that your little ones' hands, toes, and heads remain warm all winter long, and that your sanity, as it pertains to this issue, will stay in tact.

### *2. Sanity-Saving Mommy Must-Haves*

It's evident from the list above that our children require a ton of necessities while on the road. But what about us moms? There's no denying that we're in need of a few personal items ourselves to assist with our own minor emergencies while traveling to and fro. We moms need a stash of Sanity-Saving Mommy Must-Haves (SSMMH). But what goes into a kit like this? By polling my mommy friends, and wracking my own brain, here are just a few of the items you may want to keep handy in your own, personalized mommy emergency kit.

**The Bible:** Whether it's an actual Bible, a devotional, or a piece of paper with your favorite verse written on it, you need some form of Scripture somewhere in your car at all times. In fact, keep your Bible close and use it whenever you can. I mean, why take the time to refresh your Facebook status—while in line to pick up your child from school or wherever else—when you can renew your mind, soul, and spirit, instead? That Bible of yours is a life-saver, so why not put it in a place where you spend a whole lot of time?

> *"Listen for God's voice in everything you do*
> *and wherever you go;*
> *He's the one that will keep you on track."*
>
> **—Proverbs 3:6 MSG**

**Feminine hygiene items:** It always seems like the moment I find myself in need of a feminine hygiene product they've all managed to become completely useless within the confines of my purse. Usually, I find them broken in half, dislodged from the applicator, or in complete tatters at the bottom of my handbag. But in order to avoid such problems—and minimize your chances of Toxic Shock Syndrome—use a resealable bag to store your items in your own SSMMH emergency kit. This way, they will remain intact, sanitary, centrally located, and ready for use when the need arises.

**Money:** Whether it be for the parking meter, a coffee run, a charitable cause, or any other last-minute need that finds you scrambling for cash, you'll want to have some extra moola in your car. By keeping just twenty dollars—divided into various bills and change—in a separate envelope, you'll save yourself the added stress that not having exact change can create. Restock when necessary.

**Travel-size everything:** This means toothbrushes, grooming kit, shampoo/conditioner, comb, aloe vera, hair ties. You name it, and they probably make it in a travel-size option, which is perfect for your kit, because you just never know when you may need one of these items. Stock up on these sanity-savers by visiting your favorite dollar store and purchasing anything and everything you may ever need in case of a mommy emergency.

**Earplugs:** You hear what I'm screaming on this one? Sometimes the sound of silence is all a mom needs to restore her sanity. Oh, and if you're heading out on a long car trip, make sure to have a pair of these on hand and ready to use (provided that you're riding in the passenger seat, that is).

**Chocolate:** A stash of chocolate is oftentimes just what we need to help calm us down after an adventure in the mommyhood. Is this the healthiest snack option? Probably not. Is it convenient to keep in your car, especially during those hot summer months? Nope. Not at all. But let's be honest here. Sometimes nothing helps smooth over a stressful situation like a king-size candy bar, and the chocolaty goodness it's comprised of. If you're like me, then by all means, keep a small stash. Where small hands can't find it. Somewhere in your vehicle, under lock and key. Seriously. Oh, and during those months where the summer sun threatens to melt your "emergency" chocolate supply, invest in tootsie rolls, instead. They're a lot less messy but still offer that chocolate surge we may need to carry us through . . . in an emergency, of course.

**Deodorant:** How many times have we moms run out of the house forgetting to take care of ourselves in the process? Our kids may be dressed, fed, and ready for school, but on the drive there, we suddenly realize—due to the odor emanating from under our arms—that we forgot to apply deodorant? We stink and are now required to make a mad dash to the drug store before gracing anyone else with our presence. By purchasing a small, travel-size deodorant for moments such as these, you'll save yourself time, energy, and a whole lot of awkward moments. Oh, and your friends and loved ones will thank you for it.

**Extra cell phone charger:** Never leave home without one, but just in case you do, at least you'll have a backup in your kit. Smartphones need smart girls, too.

*Whew!* That certainly does seem like a lot of stuff to house in your trunk when you think about it, doesn't it, girls? But have no fear. The home improvement sections of most stores will offer plenty of solutions when it comes to packing these items within your vehicle. Simply invest in one plastic crate, don't forget the accompanying lid, and remember that this unit should be large enough to hold your items but small enough not to take up too much space within your trunk. That's really all you need. Simple, don't you think?

WARNING: Please note that maintaining, supplying, and restocking your emergency kits are extremely important tasks in order for this system to work efficiently. I mean, we're trying to create less stress here, after all. My recommendation? Pick one day of the month, perhaps the fifteenth, to update and thoroughly check the status of your kits. Word to the wise: this act must become routine. Check it once a month, every month, and you'll be oh-so-glad you did.

## The Glove Box

It seems like the glove box has become yet another area to store more stuff. In fact, there's nothing like being pulled over by an officer of the law (so I've heard) and reaching into your glove box compartment only to find candy bar wrappers, a stash of napkins, a broken tampon, coupons to the car wash . . . and an outdated/expired proof of registration. The glove box is a fairly small compartment meant for the sole purpose of storing a few key items, and not much else. Stick to these objects only and you're golden.

**Proof of insurance:** Make sure you have it, and that it's current. The police officer does not need yet another reason to write you a citation. Keep this in mind.

**Vehicle registration:** Yep, you will definitely need this as well, especially when getting pulled over for speeding way too fast in your minivan . . . again. I repeat: this is only what I've *heard*.

**Emergency contact card:** I like to have a list of emergency contacts written down and in my glove box just in case something happens and the responders need to know who to call, and my phone is nowhere to be found. Just an idea, girls.

**Emergency life-saving gadget:** I have seen way too many news clips, movies, and *Dateline* episodes where someone has become trapped in the confines of their car due to a traffic accident. For me—and the anxiety that the aforementioned shows have caused me—I need reassurance that if my car suddenly becomes submerged in a lake, pond, ocean, or any other pool of water, I will be able to rescue all occupants of my car safely and quickly. I also know if this were to happen, the superhuman strength I like to think I would possess under the circumstances may or may not be called into action. Instead, the best backup plan would be to invest in tools like the LifeHammer, which can literally cut through glass and seatbelts at lightning speed, and provide me with the sense of security I need on the road. Invest in one of these tools for your own peace of mind, and keep it in your glove box at all times..

So, now that you have a better idea of what your car should have and not have, it's time to discuss taking care of that ride of yours. Hey, a car is a pretty big investment that immediately begins depreciating upon exiting the dealership. Might as well invest a little bit of your time and effort now making sure that it runs right, rather than losing your moola later.

## MINIVAN MAINTENANCE

This is crazy, but after purchasing a vehicle, it appears that the proud new owner is expected to take care of it as well—as in bathing, cleaning, fueling, and making sure that it's operating correctly. I'll be the first to admit that part of the reason I purchased a minivan in the first place was due to its reputation of being ultra-reliable. But, whether your car is low maintenance or not, upkeep is definitely required if you want to ensure minimal breakdowns in the future. Like everything else we own, we've got to take care of our vehicles, too. While restocking and inspecting your emergency storage stash each month, why not add this small list to the mix and maintain the following on your car?

### The Checklist:

- ☆ Check the service date of your car (last oil change), and take care of it if necessary.
- ☆ Check your tires. If they look like they might be low on air, fill 'em up.

- ☆ Check your emergency supply kits. Are they up to date? Restock as needed.
- ☆ Clean your car out of old receipts, drinks, wrappers, toys, and other randomness that tends to accrue.
- ☆ Vacuum your vehicle.
- ☆ Wash your car. Including the inside, and especially the rear windows that have now become a vice for your children to play Tic-Tac-Toe on.

Yep. There's no denying that our vehicles have become our homes on wheels. And as most of us moms can attest to, once our kids reach a certain age, we spend the majority of our time chauffeuring them back and forth between school, functions, and a slew of other activities. But by incorporating the tips I've given you, by equipping your cars with all the necessities I've mentioned, and by implementing a schedule to maintain your vehicle and its contents, those days of crazed chaos within your car might be long gone. You'll be the mom who's equipped and completely capable of tackling any minor emergency while on the road—primed and ready with her supplies in tow, and an inner calm that can only come from being one seriously prepared mama.

Still have junk in the trunk?

Not you, Wonder Woman Wannabes.

Not anymore.

3

# FRAZZLED AND FRUSTRATED—THIS MAMA'S STRESSED OUT

*"I call as my heart grows faint;*
*lead me to the rock that is higher than I."*

**–Psalm 61:2**

No matter how many sanity-saving tips I provide, one thing is for certain: as women, wives, and mommies in today's world, we're going to get stressed out from time to time—or maybe a whole lot of the time. Unfortunately for some of us, it manages to happen much more often than we'd like and serves as a reminder that we're wading through the trenches of motherhood. Well, they're not for the faint of heart. Stress is simply our bodies' way of saying, "Girl, you've got too much going on right now and may be in serious need of slowing down . . . and soon."

But we're moms, and slowing down is something many of us don't know how to do. From the moment our feet hit the floor each morning, our lives are seemingly inundated with stressful situations. Before we can even reach for that first cup of coffee, we're already running in a million different directions attempting to get our kids ready, our days figured out, and our routines well under way. Let's face it: each of us takes on the jobs and responsibilities of many. And whether invited or not, stress has landed a starring role smack-dab in the middle of our lives. We're busy . . . and maybe we're too busy for our own good.

But what is stress and why do we let it consume us so entirely?

Don't worry. I won't bore you with a long-winded, science-infused, detailed reading from the dictionary to describe what's going on in our brains during these moments of possible implosion. I'm not looking to provide you with a technical answer anyway. Rather, my focus throughout this chapter is to figure out how to deal with the pressures placed upon us by our children, our society, and most importantly, ourselves. By exposing the triggers of our stress and providing methods to properly deal with it, hopefully, we can exit this roller coaster ride of negativity once and for all.

Buckle your safety belts.

## LIFE IN THE FAST LANE

"That's why we pray just to make it today," I began to sing as images from the early '90s—and the era of MC Hammer—flashed through my mind. I was really enjoying listening to that song and couldn't help but croon loudly as I sped along in my minivan on the way to pick up my children from school. I was excited to see them, eager to learn about their days, and anticipated spending some much-needed family time that evening once we returned home.

But that was before I actually picked them up from school.

As soon as they got in the car, the scene I had envisioned in my mind played out much differently in real life: the fights began, the tattling started, and the screaming ensued. In just minutes, I had gone from a woman singing the praises of my blessings (well, as much as that MC Hammer song would allow) to a mother completely consumed by the wrath her children were creating in the backseat. Those moments of feeling like the luckiest mom on earth quickly turned to feeling like a helpless victim, plagued by unruly children exhibiting horrendous behavior. And if this wasn't bad enough, my three-year-old, who has impeccable timing I might add, professed at that precise moment that he had indeed just pooped his pants on top of everything else that was transpiring around me. As the ventilation within our minivan grew thick with odor, my kids couldn't help but claw at the windows, gasping for fresh air. And it appeared I was headed for a major mommy meltdown.

I was annoyed, frustrated, and angered by my children. They couldn't make it five minutes without arguing, yelling, or instigating some type of kiddie fiasco. They couldn't keep their hands to themselves, even though they'd been lectured on the importance thereof too many times to count. And, in addition to the havoc being wreaked in my minivan by my older two children, my youngest just couldn't be left out, nor outdone. As if all of this wasn't bad enough, I was also dealing with a nasty case of pooped-in toddler pants.

So much for that peaceful night at home I was looking forward to. So much for my sanity.

This episode represents just *one* example of the daily battles that can rage within our homes—or our cars for that matter—causing undue amounts of stress, and a war of wills we're simply too tired to fight anymore.

Take note moms, because this is where vigilance is required. If we're not careful, situations like these can deprive us of our basic desire to experience joy in our privileged role as mothers. Whether we like it or not, stressful situations will occur, just as moments of mayhem are going to take place. But we need to find a way to handle these mounting pressures in the most appropriate way possible. It's up to us to recognize these feelings for what they are and make the concerted effort to not displace them upon our children. It's within our power to control our tongues, still our minds, and call on the Holy Spirit. Let's lean on God for help and understand that the stress occurring within our lives is meant to be shared with our Creator, not handled by ourselves.

So, how are we supposed to "deal" with nerve-wracking moments when our faces turn red with anger, steam is about to blow out of our ears, and our heads are threatening to turn around in circles—resembling the nightmarish image of Linda Blair from so many years ago? It's in instances like these that we need to step away from the chaos entrapping us, and take a much-needed break from the situation.

What I'm trying to say is when you feel negativity consuming you to the point where it's all you can see, think, and feel, then it's time for a rest, a time-out if you will.

## "T" IS FOR TIME-OUT

Just as our tumultuous toddlers need time to cool down from the rage that battles within them (hello, tantrums!), mommies are much-deserving of the same type of rest. Every once in a while, we're in need of a mommy "do-over"—a chance to hit the reset button, to rewind our day, and possibly take back the words spoken out of anger, the frustration exhibited, or the ugliness displayed to the people we love the most. You see, even with the best intentions, stressed-out mommies have a tendency to become agitated earlier, annoyed faster, and model a behavior that doesn't necessarily embody the image of Christ, nor the definition of patience. But rather than beating ourselves up over it, we've got to take action against it. Raising children is stressful, but let's be honest: no one ever claimed it was going to be easy.

We're human, which means we're going to get discouraged, have bouts with frustration and times where we're in serious danger of going off the deep end. Maybe you've yelled at your kids, treated them disrespectfully, or just had a moment that you're not too proud of. It happens; and chances are, it's probably going to happen again.

But here are a few tips to help keep your calm, and hopefully, reduce your stress level.

**Pray:** Pray hard and pray often when you're on the verge of "losing it." God already knows what lies in our hearts, but His delight comes in hearing it from our lips. Ask Him for strength and inner peace, and that these moments of complete and total anarchy will pass . . . and soon! Pray for wisdom to handle such situations, and for patience to endure them. Finally, pray for your children by name, and pray out loud in the hope that they will embrace the peaceful attitude you yourself could use at this very moment.

> *"Be joyful in hope, patient in affliction,*
> *faithful in prayer."*
>
> **—Romans 12:12**

**Pause:** I know I've mentioned this before, but prior to acting out in anger or shouting with rage, remember to pause. In doing so, you're much more likely to curb your tongue, stifle negativity, and give yourself a moment of clarity before dealing with your children.

**Call somebody.** Call your mom, a friend, your hubby, or anyone that won't mind you venting for a half hour or so. It's better to let it all out to a friend or relative than to take it out on your kiddos.

**Scream.** This type of release is best done alone in your car or another sound-proof area. This is not, and I repeat, *not* to be done toward your children, husband, the family dog, or any other living, breathing being that happens to cross your path. If you need to reduce your tension, and feel a good scream coming on anyway, run to your car, let it out, along with a good cry, and then resume your normally scheduled programming.

**Take a break.** Go to your room, lock the door, and collect your thoughts in order to calm down. Try deep, cleansing breaths, or resort to your devotional to help snap you out of the negative and back into the positive.

**Reflect.** Your kids may be driving you crazy at this particular moment, but rather than focusing on their current behavior, reflect upon their births instead.... Yes, you heard me right. Remember those moments of pure joy as you welcomed that sweet bundle into your arms? Hold onto that image, retreat to your happy place, and rejuvenate your mind and soul with positive thoughts. Believe me, an attitude of gratitude can go a long way in putting things into perspective when everything else seems to be going wrong.

**Take Inventory.** Aside from your children's behavior, other factors might be involved when it comes to high amounts of stress in your life. Maybe it's a work situation you have to deal with, a struggling relationship, financial problems, and so forth. Recognize where your stress is coming from and try and refrain from having it spill out onto your children. Easier said than done, I know.

**Seek help.** Sometimes our stress can consume us to the point where we can hardly function anymore. Depression can set in and our psyches can become somewhat debilitated. Pursuing the help of professionals who can assist in discussing and dealing with these emotions appropriately may be the answer. If you've tried the suggestions mentioned above and still harbor feelings of helplessness, it may be time to pick up the phone and call someone who can help.

So, what does all of this mean? As moms who are well aware of the blessings we've been given, we also face a number of struggles and stressful situations when it comes to raising our children. Each day can provide multiple opportunities for stress, causing inner peace to subside and anxiety to thrive. But here's the thing: no matter how demanding our situations may be, nor how often they arise, we're not, I repeat, *not*, completely helpless in how we respond to them. We have a choice when it comes to our actions, reactions, behavior, and how we carry out conflict-resolution within our families. Even better, we have the ability to replace stress with something much more powerful, and healthier, too: the Word of God.

*"Peace I leave with you; my peace I give you.*
*I do not give to you as the world gives. Do not let your*
*hearts be troubled and do not be afraid."*

**—John 14:27**

Hey, rearing children is a practice that takes a lot of patience (we're talking tons here), a lot of love, and a whole lot of faith. Take heed, Supermamas; stress will undoubtedly occur, but the love you have for your kiddos will always win out. Guaranteed.

*"I'm not telling you it's going to be easy,*
*I'm telling you it's going to be worth it."*

**–Art Williams**

# 4

# THE WANNABE'S NEED FOR CAFFEINE—AND LOTS OF IT

*"I don't have a problem with caffeine,*
*I have a problem without it."*

**—Unknown**

Picture this: you're fast asleep dreaming of distant lands, beautiful beaches, and the type of enjoyment that only complete relaxation can bring. There are no children to be seen—or heard from, for that matter—and it's as if you can literally feel the sand between your toes, as the warm sun beats down upon your face. You can smell the ocean air, feel the cool breeze brush against your skin, all while delighting in the marvelous sounds that the coastline can provide. *You are in paradise.*

Oddly enough though—and all too suddenly—you're whisked away from this serene setting by a horrible twinge of pain shooting straight through your left eye. Abruptly awakened and half out of it, you can't help but focus, with what sight you have left, on the culprit's face. Currently hovering directly above, as his chubby finger pokes your ocular cavity, sits the cute toddler you gave birth to not so long ago.

And with a grin spread wide across his face, he can't help himself from shouting: "Time to git up, mommy! . . . I awake and I hungry."

Your morning, and the next fourteen hours of your day, have officially begun, whether you were ready for them or not. It's evident from the issues you've already encountered that you're in desperate need of some caffeine (maybe intravenously), and a whole lotta prayer. You head to the kitchen as you repetitively pray for God to lighten your mood and give you the strength you're going to need to embrace the day. Oh, and if He could make sure that your coffee is plentiful and that your vision returns to normal, preferably soon, that would be ideal as well.

"Coffee will cure this," you think as you reach for your stash of home-brewed goodness, only to find an empty can instead.

Your supply of crystals has mysteriously disappeared.

"No! It can't be," you tell yourself. "Not now. Not today."

Your heart sinks, your pain worsens, and you are a mama who's seriously struggling with what to do next.

"I huuuuuuuuuuuungry," bellows that once-cute three-year-old, beckoning you to feed him, and rather impatiently.

Your hands begin to shake, your wedged-shut eye begins to twitch, and you are a Wonder Woman Wannabe going through some severe caffeine withdrawals. You beg God for a miracle in the hopes that a full canister of coffee will somehow suddenly appear. But all efforts to produce and/or find those brown beans of goodness fail. In a moment of clarity, and in the midst of your pain, you grab your whining toddler, get in the car, and proceed to the nearest Starbucks because you're a mama frantically in need of some coffee—and pronto.

However, upon your arrival, the scenario doesn't get much better...

"Give. Me. Coffee." You tell the poor girl behind the counter in an unrecognizable voice that's comes across so deep (and slightly demented) that even you're startled by the sound of it.

"Make it a venti-sized, double espresso with two pumps of whatever-you've-got-handy, and some extra whip cream. And if you've got sprinkles, I need some of those too," you bark at the young girl currently staring in disgust at your slightly hemorrhaging eye.

"Your name?" she inquires.

"Um, Judy. No, wait, it's Jessie. Sorry, my name is Jenny. Yes, it's Jenny."

With a look of confusion that screams, *I got stuck with the crazy lady and may need back-up really soon*, the barista utters, "That'll be four dollars and fifty-four cents, please," as she attempts to focus on your functioning eye, but can't help gawking at your injured one instead . . . which may be in need of some medical attention at this point.

"I'm huuuungry," your child continues to scream as a full-blown toddler hissy fit ensues and the line of people behind you are unamused by the screeching sounds echoing from your unruly child.

"And give me two chocolate chip cookies as well." Yah, cuz that's exactly what your child deserves at this moment, right? But you don't care at this point. You just want to get your coffee, get your kid and get back home.

Geesh! And all you wanted this morning was a little sleep, a bit of sanity, and a hot cup of coffee to start your day. Was that too much to ask for? Apparently it was.

## GIVE ME A BREAK

With the morning like you've had, you'd probably give your left arm, or maybe just that twitching, pain-ridden eye you're nursing, for that bittersweet jolt of joe you can't help but guzzle down without a second thought. Yep. Just like the other bajillion coffee drinkers in the world today, it appears that in order to get up and functioning each morning, most mamas require some assistance—caffeine reinforcement if you will.

Hey, rude awakenings are bound to occur when little ones are on the premises; but, in order to handle them effectively, we need a backup plan. I mean, we can't head to Starbucks each and every time we have a hankering for this liquid gold if we are trying to maintain some sort of budget, right? Besides, a daily Starbucks habit (at $4.50 per day) comes to roughly $32 per week, $137 per month, and $1,640 per year. Um, that's a lot of dollars being ingested, if you ask me. Hey, it's easy to lose sight of what you're spending when you're not keeping track of it in the first place.

But you *crave* caffeine, and you *need* coffee . . . so what's a girl to do?

## CUTTING COSTS

Coffee is pretty expensive these days, as outlined by the example above, and as consumers, we need to avoid the pitfalls that come with consuming this beverage. Rather than frequenting coffee houses like Starbucks on a regular basis, we need to implement some sort of budget when it comes to this craving—all while enjoying its goodness at the same time. Luckily, said feat can be accomplished with just a little planning on your part. And here are some tips to do just that.

**Econo-size it:** Purchase your java, whether it be gourmet or name brand, at a discount superstore and reap huge savings by avoiding full retail prices.

**Become your own barista:** Invest in a coffee maker that can produce your favorite drinks without the expensive price tag attached. Perform an online search, check out reviews, and purchase a machine that will give you the beverage you desire, the way you like it best. This simple act can equate to some significant savings, ladies. Seriously. Follow it up by locating online recipes resembling your favorite gourmet concoctions. Visit Pinterest or use Google to conduct your search and explore the many options available online. Now you can make those delicious coffee house drinks in the convenience of your own home. And believe me, the savings make it so worth it!

**Limit yourself:** Cut down your visits to your favorite local brew house, limiting them to only once a week. Plan an outing with your girlfriends, or a bible study group, and meet up there over coffee . . . but just once a week. Inhale your café au lait at home the rest of the time. Major moola can be saved!

**Get creative:** Ask for gift cards for Christmas, birthdays, or other holidays where you tend to receive gifts. Use these instead of your debit card each time you go. Hey! It will be the gift that continually gives throughout the months (and years) ahead.

**Half and half:** Why not take this opportunity to cut down on your caffeine intake? Did I just say that?! Before you skip to the next tip, just hear me out on this one: by purchasing a non-designer brand of coffee at half the caffeine and mixing it with your preferred brand, not only will you increase your savings, but you'll also cut your caffeine intake in half. Definitely a win–win situation and worth the consideration, eh?

**Reduce & reuse:** When it comes to those coffee filters, have you ever thought about reusing them? You know—in an effort to reduce excess waste and all? Besides, I don't know about you, but I detest having to change out that filter each time I make coffee, so this idea was born out of pure laziness on my part, but it's definitely worth considering. Or what about reusing the coffee grounds from the previous day while you're at it? *Gasp!* Now this just might be the ultimate in gourmet coffee no-nos, but by throwing in some fresh crystals on top of those wet, day-old ones, you can achieve the cup of joe you're in need of, all while keeping your coffee bean supply stocked a tad longer. Just an idea, ladies. Please don't shoot the messenger.

**Emergency stash:** Stash an emergency packet of coffee in a place where your husband won't find it . . . maybe just enough for one pot or even just one cup. This will prevent having to head out on emergency coffee runs and save you money, and angst, in the future.

**Cut down***:* Ever thought about cutting down on your habit? Just kidding. Wait, you're not laughing? Okay, sorry. Omit this option, accept my apologies, and carry on with your caffeine ingestion.

Let's face it. Our coffee obsessions are deliciously delightful, and for the general population of mamas, very necessary. But maybe we need to cut down on the Starbucks habit by brewing java right in our very own kitchens. Maybe we can use the tips I've mentioned to save some money and invest it elsewhere

## COFFEE TALK

Sitting down over coffee to chat with friends and/or visit with loved ones is one of our favorite things to do as a culture. It's amazing what a little coffee talk can do for the soul, isn't it? It seems to me that in those conversations, relationships can be strengthened, our minds can feel renewed, and the weight of the world can reduce its load on us, if even just for a little while. Yep. All of this can happen over a single cup of coffee. What better company is there than to take a seat and enjoy a cup of joe by gabbing with none other than God, Himself?

Just as having relationships with our loved ones is essential for us to thrive, so is having a relationship with our Lord and Savior. In fact, it holds the highest ranking of importance for each and every one of us women. We need that time with our Father. We need morning chats, midday discussions, and late night talks with the One who knows us better than we could ever know ourselves. God definitely needs to hear from us, just as we need to feel His presence within our lives on a daily basis. Coffee and the caffeine it contains will help keep us going throughout the day, but nothing, and I mean nothing, will help us feel more alive than our daily discussions with our Lord, Jesus Christ.

So brew some coffee, grab your Bible, and sit down with your Creator for a few moments each day. Nothing says starting your morning off right like a fresh cup of home-brewed goodness mixed with a warm fuzzy from our Father. And just think: no matter how rude our awakenings might be, how early they may occur, or even how many times we get poked in the eye, God will meet us when and where we need Him the most.

*With ~~coffee~~ God, anything is possible.*

# 5

# PEEING IN PEACE: UNLOCKING THE SECRET

*"I always feel like somebody's watchin' me,*
*and I have no privacy."*

**—"Somebody's Watching Me," Rockwell**

It'd been two hours since my little ones had awakened; breakfast was over, their bellies were full, and those kiddos of mine had become glued to the television watching Dora the Explorer in her latest adventures. All was calm within my home . . . and dare I say, peaceful? But I knew all of that was about to change, because I'd reached the pivotal point of my morning where that full pot of coffee—you know, the one I *thought* would be a good idea earlier—combined with the indigestion from last night's enchilada dinner had officially kicked in. Yep, my body had begun pleading with me to get to a bathroom (and quick), before an adult-sized accident was about to take place.

But I'm no stranger to what occurs when nature calls upon *this* mama. It's no surprise that in the instant I make a motion, a gesture, or even think about using the restroom, my children are able to detect it. It's their sixth sense, if you will. Like a pack of wolves tracking their prey, my kids appear front and center as the procession begins and the play date around the potty I'm perched on gets underway.

I know you know what I'm talking about.

For whatever reason, there's something about a mom using the restroom that causes her children to immediately flock to her side, as they desperately vie for her attention and mercilessly plead for her assistance. Now I, for one, can think of a slew of other bonding moments I'd prefer to enjoy with my children, rather than gathering around a latrine, just as I've also realized that any sort of private time needed in order to "take care of business" is virtually non-existent when you're a mom. It's almost as if our children take pleasure in invading our bathroom space, our dignity, and any peace we hoped to secure for just a few, short moments.

But is this the plight of all Wannabes? Or can something be done to remedy this problem and allow us mamas back into our bathrooms, alone, and without interruption?

## KIDS WILL BE KIDS

Now, I'll be honest—I was semi-prepared for some of the rude awakenings this parenting gig would provide, but I never, and I mean *never*, thought that my trips to the restroom would become chaotic at best. These days? It's all about using the bathroom as quickly as possible—as in a mad rush—before something catches fire or someone has to go to the hospital.

Yep, it's no secret that children tend to choose the most inconvenient times to manifest mayhem within our homes. Spilt milk, dirty dogs running amuck, Frisbees getting stuck on the roof, strangers at the door, and minor flesh wounds all tend to take place while we're . . . *ahem* . . . "busy." And I can't help but wonder: Should I feel fortunate that my children want to be around me all of the time? Should I embrace my restroom visitors, even though these moments seem awkward at best and kinda weird? While I'm still struggling to figure out the answers to these questions, I do know one thing for sure: most (if not all) of us moms have experienced some pretty harrowing ordeals while attempting to relieve ourselves. I've endured numerous instances myself that have left me nothing short of dumbfounded by their occurrences. Please tell me you can understand. Please tell me that even though I know how disturbing this sounds, that as moms, we can all relate to the fact that we may never pee in peace again.

Or can we?

I think it may be time to take some action.

Are you with me, ladies?

## POTTY PLANNING

When nature calls, we had better listen, because holding the contents of our bladder is just plain bad for our bodies. It should be our goal to get those toxins out, not hold them captive within our anatomy while our comfort levels dip extremely low, and we find ourselves mimicking our children's "potty dance" to ward off an accident. But, with a house full of young kids to look after, heading to the restroom can be a hard feat to manage . . . one that, believe it or not, may take some planning on your part to achieve. Oh my gosh, wait! Am I suggesting that we start planning our trips to the restroom?

Indeed I am.

But before you roll your eyes and think I've lost my mind (which could definitely be the case), let me explain what I'm talking about. It appears that kids need some sort of distraction in order to keep them safe, sound, and somewhat busy while we tend to our needs. So, how does one devise a strategy to do so and what exactly does this entail?

**Puzzling times:** Gather your brood together and pull out a five hundred piece puzzle on which all their favorite characters are displayed. Sit down with them and begin constructing this brainteaser.

Once your children are engaged, simply slip away and attend to your needs. This can probably buy you at least five minutes, give or take, without sibling uproar or other major meltdowns. Five minutes in the potty is a huge amount of time for us moms.

**"Bible Flip":** I especially love this game, because not only do I get to tend to my needs, but it also provides my older children with the opportunity to reference and read the Bible more. Choose a verse and have your children locate it within their Bibles. Have them write a brief synopsis as to what the selected verse means to them and how they can apply it to their lives. See? Deep, moving, educational, and spiritual, all while you excuse yourself for a quick moment to take care of your own needs. Divine intervention? Perhaps.

**Turn on the telly:** Yes, sometimes the TV *can* be used as a babysitter and sometimes—like in the moments when you're about to pee your pants—it's totally okay to use it in such a way. Flip on the tube and turn on the kiddos' favorite cartoon, which you may want to have stored on the DVR for times like these. Make a quick trip to the bathroom, and return feeling refreshed, relieved, and perhaps a few pounds lighter.

**Order up:** Got kids at home? Plan a potty break around snack time or right in the middle of lunch. Make sure to open their wrappers, deal out those drinks, and provide them with a napkin prior to heading for the loo.

**In-house scavenger hunt:** Type out a list of items your kids will enjoy searching for within your home. Once they've successfully located each one, they must cross the item off the list. The winner receives a prize to be decided by mom, who's recently sprung from the bathroom and feeling fresher. Believe me, this works!

**Art gallery:** Throw down some washable markers and crayons, along with a few pieces of construction paper or coloring books, and have your kids make their own masterpieces. Make it a contest, offer a prize as an incentive, and then head off to the restroom for your much-needed potty break while they get their creative juices flowing. They won't even know you're gone.

Now, I know that some of us could seriously care less if we have an entourage in tow while going about our business. In fact, some moms may have even grown accustomed to these distractions and don't find it bothersome in the least. But for the rest of us who need discretion, locating some non-chaotic restroom time by incorporating the ideas just mentioned may be the answer. Remember, you'll want to have a slew of activities at your disposal to keep your kiddos occupied—without them knowing it of course—in order to get the privacy you're desperately desiring back for good.

## THE DANGER ZONE

Reclaiming a hint of discretion isn't the only issue we moms face when heading into those bathrooms of ours. With children in our homes, the lavatory can be considered a condemned area of sorts: a place where germs can fester, puddles may form, and safety issues for mamas can arise. Sure, we may have equipped our kiddos with information on proper bathroom etiquette—such as how to take care of their business, avoid messes, and the importance of cleaning up after themselves—but sometimes (okay, *a lot* of times) our kids are in too much of a hurry to really care about the in-depth teachings we've so diligently shared with them. This is where we need to be mindful when using the same restrooms as our children. Not sure what I'm talking about? Consider these tips every time you head in for a potty break of your own:

**Look before you leak:** It's the age-old problem males (of all ages) typically possess after using the restroom. For some reason, putting the toilet seat down is an easily forgotten task for our guys. It's also completely dangerous for us ladies who aren't expecting a harsh encounter with the commode upon retreating to the bathroom. If you've got males in your home, then you must make it a practice to always look before placing your backside in the potty position.

**AIM:** As a mom, it's a no-brainer that you absolutely must check the seat *before* sitting down to make sure that your little man has accurately placed his urine into the toilet bowl, as opposed to on or around the seat you're about to sit on. Word to the wise: check for faulty aim (and the repercussions thereof) prior to resting your rump on the latrine.

**Rogue TP:** We've all managed to do this at one point or another and nothing can leave a Wannabe feeling more stranded than the realization that our toilet paper has run out. This is just one more step in accurately assessing your bathroom surroundings before doing your business. Make sure the restrooms within your homes are adequately stocked with enough toilet paper to last a week, and that you've kept some of your backup stash within reach. And don't forget to check and recheck those bathrooms that are used more frequently. Better to be safe than sorry . . . or stuck on the toilet waiting for your toddler to rescue you with a fresh roll.

**Come equipped**: Every now and then, usually when my husband is home, I can sneak away for some bathroom time and take an extra five minutes. It's in these rare times that I like to look through magazines, scan through my Facebook newsfeed, update my Twitter account, and check my emails. On those infrequent occasions when you find extra time in el baño, make sure to come equipped with reading material, your cell phone, or whatever else you'd like to pass the time with for a bit. Hey, if we can score a few minutes of peace, then we had better be armed with some reading material.

My fellow mamas, peace on the potty can be yours with enough preparation and a bit of creativity. Be sure to try out these tips, be ready, and by all means, relieve your bladder as often as you can. Audience or no audience, and crazy chaos aside—when nature calls, we gals need to listen!

6

# SUPERHERO-SIZED HORMONES: BATTLING PMS

*"This too, shall pass . . ."*

As a child, I vividly remember watching a television series depicting the fictional life of one very angry superhero. I take that back—he wasn't angry. This guy was straight up belligerent. He was a man so enraged by the transpiring of certain events within his day that his body would undergo an extreme physical metamorphosis the moment his anger reached a certain level. Slightly frightened, my seven-year-old self couldn't help but stare at the image on-screen as it transformed into something almost subhuman. He became green with rage and had muscles bursting out of his clothing, as his ginormous body convulsed with crazed fury the moment his anger let loose. He was one upset dude. And as a kid, I couldn't help but feel empathy for those poor souls who'd caused him such distress in the first place, because by the end of each episode, they had paid sorely for their mistakes.

After growing into an adult woman—with fluctuating hormones no less—I have to confess that I became increasingly aware of the similarities between me and The Incredible Hulk. Now, I know that sounds like a fairly odd statement to make, so let me explain. Short of having bulging muscles, dark green skin, and a bushy unibrow, it became apparent that I possessed similar behaviors when a certain time of the month presented itself. As stereotypical as this might be, there's no refuting the effects of PMS (Pre-Menstrual Syndrome) on my life. I can get irritable, angry, impatient, and just downright horrible to be around. I'm a girl who becomes impaired by her mood, has no control over her emotions, and feels cursed by the blasted hormones I was born with.

Let's face it though: a Wonder Woman Wannabe dealing with PMS is just not a gal you want to mess with, and the reason behind that is purely scientific. PMS was first named as a medical issue in 1931, when gynecologist Dr. T. Frank gave a paper called "The Hormonal Causes of Premenstrual Tension" to a meeting of the New York Academy of Medicine. He found PMS to be a "condition characterized by a constellation of physical and emotional symptoms that have an impact on a woman's day-to-day activities."

Um, ya think?! Seriously though, after reading that PMS is a legitimate disorder and not just some excuse for girly grumpiness, I can't help but feel vindicated. Certainly I don't want to be angry or irritable all of the time, but during those moments of luteal mischief, I now know that I'm at the mercy of my raging hormones and just can't help it.

Gosh, I feel bad for my kids, my husband, and anyone else I come in contact with. But there's got to be a better way, right? Aside from turning into the female version of the Hulk, we ladies need to find ways in which we can combat our craziness and remain in control. We need to figure out how to handle the conditions associated with this monthly disorder, and still deal with our families in ways that don't scream, "Cross my path and pay the price!" Short of going into hiding or secluding ourselves from society in general, what can we do to free ourselves of those not-so-fun female problems?

I might just have your answer.

## DISORDERLY CONDUCT: HOW TO DEAL

> *"Commit your way to the Lord; trust in him and he will do this: He will make your righteousness shine like the dawn, the justice of your cause like the noonday sun."*
>
> **—Psalms 37:5**

What's a girl to do when she's tired, fairly crazy emotional, and suffering from a semi-severe case of PMS? Well, short of going into hiding for seven days, we can relieve some of those nasty symptoms associated with our time of the month by trying some—if not all—of these ideas to remain calm and carry on:

**Take a hot bath**: Just fifteen minutes of uninterrupted soak time will help relieve some of the pain associated with your period and PMS. Now, for a mom in high demand, fifteen minutes may seem a little tough to fit into a busy schedule, so this may be the time to seek out some help, girls. Ask a spouse, relative, friend, or anyone else to watch your kiddos for just a few minutes while you indulge in a much-needed bath. Or better yet, wait until the kids are in bed and take as long as you want to help rid yourself of those pesky PMS symptoms. The heat will not only provide relief to those muscles surrounding your period-producer, but give you the time needed to relax and recharge.

**Incorporate essential oils:** Talk about relaxing—how about throwing some calming lavender in your bath or using other essential oils to help get you through this monthly, mood-swingin' time? Check out your local health/supplement store for all the latest info and news surrounding essential oils. And, as always, make sure to contact your medical provider for additional information prior to implementing anything new into your bathing regimen.

**Listen to music**: Contemporary Christian music always lifts my mood and helps me focus on what's most important. By slipping on your headphones, you'll find peace in the uplifting sentiments, worship, and praise.

Note: Try to steer clear of rock, metal, or any other anxiety-inducing types of music. Think uplifting, not headbanging.

**Pray**: When Mother Nature presents you with your "monthly bill," and those not-so-fun side effects that usually accompany it, by all means, *pray*! Always, and I mean always, take it to your Father, girls. He knows your struggles and is eager to be the shoulder you lean upon. Talk to Him, vent to Him, and request some relief from Him—and possibly a mood makeover if He's not too busy (hey, it's worth a shot, right?). He'll help you out, and better yet, He'll be glad that you came to Him when in need.

**Use visual reminders:** Sometimes a visual reminder might be all you need to help snap you out of your negative mood and back into the land of positive thinking. Simply use a sticky note—or billboard if you need it—and try posting something along these lines: "Keep Calm: It's Not You, It's Those Horrible Hormones." Because even though you're irritable and your hormones are outta whack, this phase of your cycle doesn't define who you are. So go ahead and remind yourself of your "awesomeness," and keep in mind that when it comes to your period . . . this too shall pass.

**Stick to a healthy diet**: As much as we may crave chocolate, cookies, cake, pie, candy bars, or any other unhealthy product during this time of the month, it's best to stick to a healthy diet, rich in fruits, veggies, and proteins. For me, I like to stock-up on protein bars that mimic the taste of chocolate in order to trick myself (and my cravings) into believing that I'm eating candy, when in reality, I'm consuming something much better for me. Works every time.

Want another tip? When devising your meal plan each month, keep the week of your period in mind and stock up on healthy snacks, keeping those binging issues in mind. Oh, and always remember to take your vitamins—after speaking to your doctor of course—and maintain a regular supplement routine, too. Word to the wise.

**Guzzle some H2O**: Most of us tend to feel a bit "puffy" when suffering from PMS. Water retention is yet another issue faced leading up to and during our periods. But as it turns out, guzzling *more* water each day will actually help in fighting off this bloating effect. Who knew? Water is also an extremely important component in proper hydration (we're in need of eight, eight-ounce glasses per day) and will help ward off that "empty feeling" that tends to plague our bellies at this time.

**Exercise:** Exercise?! You mean I'm expected to run, climb stairs, and jump up and down while suffering from the symptoms of PMS? Yes. . . . Well, sort of. I wouldn't necessarily recommend jumping up and down or engaging in acrobatics, but getting your body out of the fetal position and into the gym for a little bit of exercise will definitely do a girl, and her grumpiness, some good. By exercising, your body will release endorphins, which are crucial in calming the negative vibes you're currently emoting. Not only that, exercise is good for you, so go for a walk, ride your bike, exert some type of physical energy to help offset your discomfort and stabilize your mood.

**Sleep more**: Despite what your nightly routine may be—mine involves everything from scrapbooking to catching up on my favorite TV shows—the majority of us girls have bodies desperately in need of eight hours of sleep, at least. Our physiques are in a constant state of motion all day long, and by the time night falls, we're in serious need of some major Zs. Don't deprive your body of the rest it needs, and do your best to get to bed as early as possible. Besides, isn't that why DVR was invented?

Along with employing healthy habits during your menstrual cycle, you're also going to want to resist some unhealthy ones. As I've stated before, our hormones are all over the place, slightly unpredictable, and, when it comes to our periods, seem to be in control. Take note and try to avoid the following:

**Sugar binges**: I'm a girl who is a sucker for chocolate: milk chocolate, semi-sweet chocolate, white chocolate, and even hot chocolate. Undoubtedly, I have a serious weakness in willpower when it comes craving sweets during my "special" time of the month. If you can relate, then listen up, because as it turns out, giving in to junk food binges will in fact have a negative effect on our blood sugar levels, causing them to spike very high and then come crashing down just as fast. Know what this means for us? I-R-R-I-T-A-B-I-L-I-T-Y . . . and lots of it.

We certainly don't need to foster any more of that, now do we?

So what's a girl with a serious addiction to chocolate supposed to do in times like these? Well, if you're in dire need of a chocolate product—or ten—try indulging in dark chocolate or raw cacao, instead. These have the magnesium that our bodies want. Most other types of chocolate have already been processed and left devoid of this nutrient. So, if you're craving something chocolaty and aren't interested in another protein bar, enjoy a few pieces of dark chocolate if you'd like. Bon appetit.

**Aggression:** How many of you have ever seen the watermelon-bashing comedian known as Gallagher? I'll be honest, when PMS rears its ugly head and I'm suffering from some of its major symptoms, I would love nothing more than to be that guy for the day—or maybe even just an hour or so.

But, this probably isn't the best idea, now is it?

As the mom of the house, bashing an inanimate object could indeed provide temporary relief, but it would also require to me to clean up after myself and the huge mess I made. This act would only add to my fury, not take it away. Besides, this type of disturbing behavior might also welcome looks from the neighbors, and possibly an intervention or two from family members. So let's use another tactic besides aggressive reinforcements to relieve our frustration and irritability. Try a stress ball, or re-read all the tips I've listed above and eat that watermelon instead of pulverizing it. Much better, don't you think?

**Sad, sappy, chick-flicks**: Don't get me wrong, I love a good chick-flick and would love nothing more to indulge in a marathon of romantic movies all day long if given the choice. But when dealing with PMS, the last thing you want to do is watch a movie that will cause the tears to flow and the heartache to linger. Add that to the irritability experienced when you realize that your hubby in no way acts like the sensitive, macho main character in the film, and that innocent chick-flick instantly becomes a recipe for disaster. Avoid the sap, and indulge in a comedy, instead. Remember, you want to lighten your mood, not cause it to darken even more.

*"Refrain from anger and turn from wrath;*
*do not fret—it leads only to evil."*

**–Psalm 37:8**

Hey, PMS and the period that follows are certainly not the highlight of our month, but we don't need to give it any more control over us than it already has. By incorporating the to-dos and what-not to-dos I've provided, we can embrace this time a little bit better, and not rip the heads off of our loved ones in the process. And that, my friends, is a good thing!

# 7

# JESUS, TAKE THE WHEEL— THIS GIRL'S OUTTA CONTROL!

*"Jesus take the wheel, take it from my hands,*
*cause I can't do this on my own."*

**—"Jesus, Take the Wheel," Carrie Underwood**

A few weeks before my husband and I were set to be married, and as I was in the final stages of preparing our wedding plans, I came up with what I thought to be a fabulous idea—to send out itineraries to each of the attendants who made up our wedding party. It was a schedule of sorts, complete with the times and places they needed to be on our big day. Basically, with the information I was providing, everyone would know the who, what, when, where, and why during the eighteen-plus hours that would transpire over the course of this special event.

I thought I was being helpful, not controlling.

That was until one of our groomsmen emailed my hubby-to-be to ask him if there was a moment during the day in which he might be able to take a potty break. He didn't see a spot on the itinerary for one and was hoping I could make an allowance in the schedule "in case he had to go."

I couldn't help but laugh, but that's when it hit me that maybe, just maybe, I had a bit of a control issue.

*Okay!* I'll fess up and claim that throughout most of my life I've been what others commonly refer to as a "control freak," whether I've intended to be one or not.

As a Christian, I know better. But as a Wonder Woman Wannabe who's in charge of planning meals, appointments, activities, and schedules throughout the day for her family, being freakishly controlling often seems necessary. But I know that the safety and security I seek to fulfill through people, places, and things can never be fully realized for the simple reason that I am not God.

None of us is.

Just as none of us is in control.

As scary as that might sound, there's also a reassuring sense of freedom knowing that we're not in charge, we're never alone, and that the peace we seek to secure by attempting to control the environment around us just doesn't exist. Our inner peace can't come from a clean home, an organized closet, or even a completed load of laundry. It doesn't come from watching Wonder Woman re-runs, buying a new pair of shoes, or eating a delicious meal.

Nope. Inner peace originates from the Lord above, Jesus Christ, Himself.

> *"The Lord will fight for you; you need only to be still."*
>
> **—Exodus 14:14**

And as hard as it may be to dismiss our issues with control, every Wonder Woman Wannabe must learn to surrender to the One who created us, the One who knows us even better than we know ourselves. Our identity resides in Him, girls . . . not in the broom, the mop, the disinfectant spray, or the vacuum. Your identity isn't even in the children you raise or the husband you accompany. Your identity is in Him, and Him only.

You see, we weren't meant to do this job alone. God did not create mankind in His image just to cast us aside, only to meet us on the flipside, when our lives came to pass. God breathed life into every single one of us, and all He asks in return is that we set aside some quiet time with Him and obediently submit to whatever His will might be for our lives.

So maybe it's finally time we lose control—or our issues with it at least—and start stepping out in our faith, instead.

Let's surrender, place one foot in front of the other, get immersed in our Bibles, and commit to a weekly date with our parish. It's time to make the effort to get spiritually sound, so let's start by getting ourselves, and that sweet family of ours, off to church and headed in the right direction. Let's actively pursue God on a daily basis and do a little soul-searching while we're at it.

Amen?

## GETTIN' TO THE CHURCH ON TIME

*"Church is who we are, not where we go."*

**—Jarrid Wilson**

If anything makes me feel less like the Wonder Woman I'm itching to be, it's showing up late to Sunday morning service with my unruly and slightly agitated family in tow. For me, each and every Sabbath can be a bit of a struggle to get my kids fed, clothed, out of the house, and off to church on time. Come Sunday morning—amongst the groans and complaints—my children eventually rise, as we attempt to look presentable heading out the door and off to worship.

But let me tell you—it's a struggle. Each and every Sunday.

The five-minute car ride to church isn't much better either, because my children can't help but pick a fight with one another. Screams ensue and the yelling begins, leaving everyone in a pretty foul mood, on edge, and not in the best mindset to start our morning praise session.

Once inside the parish doors, not much changes. In fact, it's a mad rush for my husband and I to get our children off to their Sunday school classes and still make it into the sanctuary before Communion begins. But my Sunday morning trials aren't over yet—not for this Wonder Woman Wannabe. It's at this point that my daughter finds fault with her outfit, and how—in the twenty-five minutes since she's placed it on her body—it's now become the itchiest, ugliest, and most uncomfortable thing she owns. My middle child has started complaining that in the time it has taken to walk through those church doors, his feet have grown tired, his bones sore, and his body weary. In fact, he's not sure whether he can make it to his class, let alone through the next hour of worship. And then there's my youngest. A little boy who's always smiling (in between tantrums), and could care less if he's late to church. In fact, all this boy wants to do is make a giant leap for the parish stairs to run the toy car that has magically emerged from his pants pocket up and down the banister, walls, and carpet where other church-goers tread.

If you haven't already guessed, we are so *that* family. The family that you can't help but notice (and stare at) each Sunday morning as they arrive to church late and in complete disarray. We're the family that makes you feel better about your own Sunday morning situation. Yep. That's us—the Pig-Pens of the worship scene.

So, by the time my kids are dropped off and I'm finally able to sit down and spend some time with Jesus, I'm a frazzled, stressed-out, slightly haggard mom who finds herself praying for relief and some rest from the weariness of motherhood.

Does any of this sound familiar?

Have no fear, Wonder Mamas, because thankfully there are some ways you can cut down on the morning chaos that ensues each time you rise for another Sunday session of worship. If you're struggling with some of the same issues I have, here are some great stress-relieving tips:

**Get prepared the night before.** If it's borderline insanity trying to get your gang showered and dressed each Sunday morning, try doing it the night before. By preparing their church clothes and having everyone bathe in advance, you may just alter their negative morning moods for the better. This goes for mom and dad, too. Anything you can do the eve before will only help your efforts come Sunday morning. Oh, and don't forget to locate your gang's Bibles while you're at it. Make sure you've got everything primed and ready to go, and you might just see the difference a little preparation can make in your family's attitude. Amen!

**Do the A.M. "Amens."** Start your morning off right with some family prayer time. Gather together (mom and dad's bed works just fine), and begin by asking God for strength, followed by attitudes of patience and gratitude as you start this morning off together. This may just be what your family needs in order to get their moods and their minds headed in the right direction—up!

**Don't skip.** Skipping is for rocks, not church. Hey, it's pretty easy to come up with an excuse to miss Sunday services, but this is where the routine you're trying to keep on track can get thrown off. Make a pact with your family to place church and God Himself above any other activity. Not sports, tournaments, clinics, or even Sunday morning cartoons. God comes first; it's as simple as that.

**Work out worship times.** Pick a time to worship that will best work for your family's schedule. Most churches offer numerous service times—some even on Saturday night—in addition to their Sunday morning praise sessions. So, if the Sabbath finds you struggling to get to the church on time, check into worshipping at a different time of day, or different day altogether. See what works better for and meets the needs of your family.

**A FAMILY THAT PRAYS TOGETHER, STAYS TOGETHER.**

> *"I remember my mother's prayers*
> *and they have always followed me.*
> *They have clung to me all my life."*
>
> **—Abraham Lincoln**

Going to church isn't about, well, just going to church. It's not about serving your time each and every Sunday and then doing your own thing the rest of the week. Going to church is all about spending time with the Lord. It's about community, fellowship, discipleship, love, learning, worship, service to one another . . . and let's be real here, it's about eternity. Church may be where we go on the weekends, but it should definitely not be the only time during our week that we spend time with God. Uh-oh, I feel another item about to be added to the "to-do" list, don't you?

Spending time with God each and every day isn't a task, ladies. It's an opportunity. As moms with crazed schedules, we have to make time with Him each day, be focused on His Word, His will, and His plans for our lives. You see, our "to-do" list begins *after* we spend time with God each morning. Don't think you can swing it? Wonder Woman Wannabes, you must realize that this is what matters the most—where our chaos meets comfort, and our restlessness meets peace. This is where God meets us in our mess—and hallelujah for that!

But I know what you're saying right about now: "I must make time for Jesus, but when, where, and most importantly, how?" Seek and ye shall find, precious mamas.

**Wake up fifteen minutes earlier.** For a night owl like me who manages most of my busy work *after* my family is fast asleep, fifteen minutes of additional morning siesta time is crucial to the rest of my day. But, then again, so is tending to my spiritual needs. As I see it, I need this time with God and like to imagine His take on all of this.

Think about it for a minute: Can you see Him up there, waiting for us to rise, knowing that the least we can do—you know, for the One who gave it all—is give Him just fifteen measly minutes of our time in prayer with Him? When I think of it that way . . . His desire to spend time with me . . . somehow, waking up a few minutes early for some morning praise doesn't seem like a big deal after all. And what better way to start off the day than with a little one-on-one time with God?

**Get into the groove.** The God Groove that is. By investing in a devotional (may I recommend *Jesus Calling* by Sarah Young) and starting each and every day out with some quiet time between you and your Creator, you will definitely feel the rewards and benefits. The mayhem you're entangled with might become easier. The patience you're struggling to possess may become more virtuous. That restless soul of yours may indeed turn peaceful. Because those moments spent in prayer allow you the opportunity to bring all of your troubles, worries, and weariness right before the Lord. This is the time where you can learn the meaning of true comfort, strength, and trust. But in order to receive all of this, and more, you must devote time to God each and every day. Once you've established a daily routine, you'll never want to miss out on it again. Guaranteed!

**Pray throughout your day.** Hey, I'm a mom who prays incessantly—as in all of the time, as in I-might-have-OCD-when-it-comes-to-my-prayer-time kind of praying. If I know one thing, there is some serious power in prayer, girls. And as a woman who believes this with all of my heart, I spend a lot of time requesting that God mold me into the type of mother I desperately long to be. I pray all of these things throughout the course of my day as a way to ask for help, seek guidance, and rely on God to get me through. These moments also provide me the opportunity to draw closer to my Savior during times when I think I may just explode. Take heed, Wonder Mamas, and understand that praying most definitely prevents imploding.

**Rock on, Christian mama.** I'm not sure if you've realized this yet or not, but that minivan of yours is a worship-mobile on wheels. No, seriously! For me and my family, we find that the best time to sing songs of praise is in the car. By tuning our radio to the local Christian station, we're able to rock out, relieve stress, and uplift our moods. My kids love singing along to the songs played, as we discuss their lyrics, and the meaning behind each song. Whether it's in the car, at church, or in your own home, it doesn't matter where you are; opportunities to worship present themselves throughout the day.

## PASS IT ON

*"Rejoice always, pray continually,*
*give thanks in all circumstances;*
*for this is God's will for you in Christ Jesus."*

**—1 Thessalonians 5:16–18**

"Our faith, our passion for Christ, and our adoration for all things biblical is a love that must be shared with others. As mothers, the first disciples of Christ we look to create should be those of our offspring. We are raising the next generation of Christ-followers, which means that every aspect of our children's journeys in faith should be focused on the truth as depicted in the Bible. This is a routine that needs to be shared, and impressed upon your sweet children, as well. Luckily, I've got tips to do just that.

**That's why we pray**: Get your days, and those of your children, started off right by spending time in prayer with them each morning. Ask God for strength, wisdom, and protection over those little guys of yours. And pray that they will, in turn, honor God in everything they do. Include Scripture in their lunchboxes, along with notes of encouragement and love. Follow this up at dinnertime with prayers of gratitude and appreciation. Teach them that one can never pray enough, and to pray hard and pray often.

**Word up!**: The use of chalkboards within the home are all the rage these days, aren't they? Well, why not use one of these fun boards as a means to present Scripture to your children each and every week? Every Monday (or Sunday night if you plan ahead), select a verse from the Bible and spend the rest of the week committing those words to memory as a family. Discuss this verse daily. Ask your children questions about the meaning behind the words selected and how they can be applied to each of your lives. Get your kiddos discussing God, memorizing Scripture, and get them further in touch with their spiritualty.

**Daily devotionals**: I've already mentioned praying together, but investing in a devotional geared toward your children is yet another way that they can further their walks with God. Devotionals such as these are not only age-appropriate, but can assist your child with exploring biblical passages in depth and applying them accordingly. Go online or visit a Christian bookstore near you for your best options when it comes to purchasing a children's devotional.

**Hump day hallelujahs**: Obviously, Wednesday is smack-dab in the middle of our calendar week, which makes it the perfect night to bring your family together to spend some time with one another. After homework is done and dinner is finished, after baths have been taken and the kids are winding down (yah, right), use this designated time to play games, watch a movie, pray, or anything else that strikes your fancy. Heat up some popcorn, sip on some hot cocoa, and make it a night your kids can look forward to experiencing each and every week. They'll relish the moments spent together as a tight-knit clan, soaking up the Word and one another.

All right , Wonder Woman Wannabes, it's time step out in your faith and trust in God, and in the path He has chosen for you. Believe me when I tell you that this road isn't going to be easy. In fact, you may find your path to be a bit bumpy and filled with too many twists and turns to count; but in the end, His plan for you will always be in your best interest. He loves you too much to do otherwise.

Trust in Him. Believe in Him. He's in control, and He's got this!

*"Hear, O Israel: The Lord our God, the Lord is one. Love the Lord your God with all your heart and with all your soul and with all your strength. These commandments that I give you today are to be on your hearts. Impress them on your children. Talk about them when you sit at home and when you walk along the road, when you lie down and when you get up. Tie them as symbols on your hands and bind them on your foreheads. Write them on the doorframes of your houses and on your gates."*

**—Deuteronomy 6:4–9**

# 8

# THE WANNABE GETS SCHOOLED

*"The more that you read,*
*The more things you will know.*
*The more that you learn,*
*The more places you'll go."*

**—Dr. Seuss**

Now, I don't know about you, but when I finished my last class in college, I had this amazing sense of relief, because it was at that moment I realized that I would never be responsible for taking another test, nor would I be bombarded with the likes of assignments, special projects, or homework of any kind, ever again. My twenty (plus) years of schooling had officially been completed and I had broken free from those pressure-filled chains of academia.

Okay, maybe that's a tad overdramatic, but you know what I mean.

The funny thing is, once my kiddos walked across the thresholds of those elementary school classrooms, the homework, class projects, assignments, and test preparation I thought I had escaped not-so-long-ago came racing back in an effort to cause me panic, a few bouts of hyperventilation, and the overwhelming sense that this Wonder Woman Wannabe was about to get schooled . . . all. . . over. . . again.

Shoot! I mean, I had *just* dismissed myself from those dreaded, harassing nightmares—you know, the ones that have us back in the classroom, taking a test we're completely unprepared for, knowing that a failing grade is looming and likely? Tell me I'm not alone in this, girls? You see, when it comes to school—and the whole learning process in general—my thoughts grow anxious from the memory of curriculums past and the completion of hundreds, if not thousands, of assignments I was forced to turn in over the years.

Gosh, I get stressed thinking about it even now. Maybe you feel the same way. But as mothers with school-aged children, we have to learn not only to embrace our roles as the educators' accomplices, but figure out how to do so effectively and efficiently (without hyperventilating), all while radiating a fabulous attitude in the process.

## CHECKIN' THE 'TUDE

> *"Whatever you do, work at it with all your heart, as working for the Lord, not for men."*
>
> **—Colossians 3:23**

So, whether you've decided to send your children to public school or private school, or teach them through homeschooling, once those off-spring of ours come of age, we've got a slew of new responsibilities to uphold as partners in their education. It's up to us to help them with their homework and ensure that all assignments, projects, reports, and papers be turned in neat, correct, and on time.

Sometimes, this specific role in parenting can be hard—as in, I-don't-have-a-clue-as-to-what-the-answer-is-and-don't-want-my-kids-thinking-I'm-dumb kind of hard. Sometimes it can add stress to our days as we get bogged down with yet another assignment we've got to complete, but let's get one thing straight, girls: the education of our children is of utmost importance, which means we've got to embrace their schoolwork and set up a plan of attack in order to get it done quickly and correctly while preserving our sanity all at the same time.

Makes sense, right?

But I'll be the first to admit how easily aggravated I can become with approaching deadlines and what seems to be an all-too-consuming curriculum. As sad as this might be to admit, as a Christian mama, there have been way too many instances where I've found myself grumbling, mumbling, and sighing in exasperation at the mere mention of schoolwork. There have been plenty of times where I have balked at the opportunity to help my children with their assignments, all because I was too busy tending to my own chores. I mean, who does that? Well, unfortunately I have—which makes this next statement even more important. Ladies, don't underestimate our children's perception of us, and their awareness of our attitudes, our reactions, and the way we approach different aspects of our lives. They see the eye-rolls, they hear those sighs, and they pick up on the stress we succumb to . . . and then? Then they repeat those behaviors. Oy!

Our attitude as it pertains to our children's schoolwork is simply everything, so let's figure out a system that works for us *and* our children, shall we?

## IT'S ELEMENTARY MY DEAR GIRL: THE HOMEWORK RULES

**Establish a homework routine.** Structure is key when it comes to implementing a homework schedule. Establish a routine that your children can follow when tackling their schoolwork. Upon returning home from school each day, give your child a snack, discuss their day, and then jump them headfirst into the daily routine by confronting their first homework assignment. By doing this early enough in the evening, it will not only allow for enough time to achieve all that needs to be done, but it also will give your family the time they desire to spend together. Stick to a homework routine and reap the benefits that only structure can bring.

**Set guidelines.** Kids aren't huge fans of homework. If they know they're able to watch television or play outside once it's over and done with, more than likely, they will breeze through the assignments without attempting their best work or checking for accuracy. In fact, at times, they could care less about whether they're producing high quality or neatly presented work, eventually creating some bad habits that will be pretty hard to break later on. Make sure your children are aware of your expectations when it comes to their schoolwork. Help them to understand that, upon the completion of their homework, "rewards" will not be awarded unless they've met the criteria you've laid out for them.

**Understand your child's learning style.** There are many different ways children can learn. I, for instance, am a visual learner, while my son embraces an auditory style of learning. This can create difficulties when assisting him in solving problems related to his schoolwork. Take the time to understand the methods of learning each of your children relates to most. Look into valuable resources both online and at your local library. Speak to your children's teachers for some helpful hints and ideas in order to support your kiddos and their learning in the most effective way possible.

**Seek support.** Open communication with your children's teachers is instrumental in the learning process. I mean, I want to know everything about the dynamics of the classrooms my kiddos are enrolled in. I want to know how they're doing both academically and socially, if there are areas in need of improvement, and so forth. Hey, teachers aren't in the business of biting—nor are they as intimidating as they once were when we were kids—so as a parent, make sure to develop an open line of communication with your kids' instructors.

**Get organized.** Preparation is key, because in all honesty, no one enjoys sitting down to do homework only to realize that the ruler, glue, pen, pencil, or paper required for the assigned task is nowhere to be found. This causes stress (mostly in us), as we waste valuable time searching for these lost but oh-so-necessary items needed to complete our kiddos' coursework. Problems such as these can be avoided by setting up a homework station in your house—a zone consisting of a drawer, cabinet, or tote—that will serve as a permanent residence for all of your children's school supplies. You'll be glad you did, seriously.

**Open door policy.** I don't know everything. There, I said it. But my job as a parent is to create a welcoming environment when my children are in need of assistance, whether I know all of the answers or not. As their mom, I want my children to feel safe, secure, and supported in their academic endeavors. Even if my daughter's third grade math problems have surpassed my level of comprehension, already, it doesn't change the fact that I still want her to reach out to me when she's struggling. So, no matter if we Wonder Mamas are in the midst of making dinner, talking on the cell phone, or doing the laundry, our kids (and their schoolwork) should always take priority. Everything else comes second.

**Rejoice.** Wait, what? You heard me, girls. In those times when we might go bonkers with the amount of homework consuming our nights, take a moment to lead with your heart and not your brain. Realize that your children are coming to you for help because they need you, they trust you, and most importantly, they love the heck out of you. Lead with the love that comes from your soul, not the frustration that's brewing in the back of your mind. And if you find yourself crazed by the copious amount of schoolwork that consistently finds its way in front of you, pray—and tap into that heart of yours just a little bit more. The result will be well worth it.

All right, now that we've gotten serious for a moment, and established some guidelines and imposed some sort of structure when it comes to homework and the assistance thereof, let's delve into some other topics associated with our children's education.

Allow me to come clean here by first confessing that I happen to be a Wannabe who enjoys indulging in a class project from time to time. Yep. When my children are in need of parental supervision and assistance, it becomes abundantly clear that I have some major self-control issues when it comes to their projects. Certain class assignments can cause my eyes to glaze over with excitement as my head's sent spinning, overflowing with an abundance of craft-tastic ideas my children may or may not want to implement. I'm not sure whether it's the smell of the glue, the texture of the cotton balls, or the durability of the Popsicle sticks, but there's something about a special assignment that sends this mommy into a frenzied crafting state where I can't help but channel my sweet, art-loving elementary days of old.

But extreme caution must be exerted in times like these, because more often than not, moms like us can find ourselves overextending our aid. After all, as women who constantly seek perfection, this characteristic can sometimes take over when our children least want it to.

Don't believe me? Want proof? Don't say I didn't warn you.

## THE DIORAMA DIVA

"Hey mom," my daughter inquired on our ride home from school late last year. "Mrs. Carter sent home a notice today describing a project we have to do."

I could have sworn I was experiencing déjà vu at that moment considering "we" had just turned in a project late last week.

"Really, sweetie," I replied, in the most positive voice I could muster. "What is it and when is it due?" I probed, hoping and praying that her response would not indicate a twenty-four-hour window of time to accomplish this feat.

"In about a week. It's called a Di-a? Di-o . . ."

"DIORAMA!" I shouted, finishing her sentence as my demeanor immediately perked up with anticipation. This was a project I could get on board with—one that I had been waiting a long time for. I mean, the thought of constructing a diorama immediately took me back to my fifth grade social studies class and the scene I concocted using a shoebox, tissue paper, and some plastic figurines to showcase the great state of Connecticut.

"Ooooh, Annie . . . what's the subject and scene we you have to recreate?" I asked inquisitively.

"Umm, it's on the Chumash Indians." She spoke hesitantly as a look of fear brushed over her face—somewhat confused by my level of excitement.

"Indians!" I shouted. "This is going to be so much fun; I can hardly wait. We can make teepees and spears. Ooh, I can make a replica of Sacajawea out of clay . . . wait, was she a Chumash? Oh, who cares, this will be a blast!"

By the look on my daughter's face, I knew I had said too much. She was now dreading this project, aware that my creative juices were overflowing, and that the ideas I was going to conjure up would indeed be numerous.

You see where this is headed, right?

As soon as we got home, construction was well under way as my daughter's assignment became my own. I couldn't help but submit to my perfectionist tendencies and managed to take over. The result? An interactive diorama featuring trees, lakes, and all other resources indigenous to the assigned timeframe. There were wigwams, teepees, and specific details relating to the history my daughter was giving a synopsis on. It was beautiful I must say . . . and totally looked like something an adult had made instead of a third grade child! I was a mom who had just failed the most important assignment rule of all: the parents don't complete the projects. The kids do.

Talk about an epic mommy fail!

But hey, even moms with the best intentions can make mistakes, right? And sometimes the lessons one gleans from certain situations can benefit the parents more than the children they're raising. I'm happy to report that the Diorama Diva was laid to rest that day. And as much as this mom loves a good craft every now and then, I've realized my daughter's class projects should never become the target I force my crafting skills upon. Let's just say I've learned a few things from my days as an elementary school mom, especially the practical advice and tips I've come across the hard way—for me, there seems to be no other route.

## A+ ADVICE

Classroom assignments, homework, standard curriculums, and dealing with all things school-related can be tough on top of everything else you've got going on as a mom. But if you have kids in school and are looking for some successful ways to deal with the challenges involved and alleviating stress, then you might just want to read the following.

**Save the date.** Take out your monthly calendar. Update your cell phone. Use whatever method works best as a means of organization. Make time to sit down at the beginning of each week and input upcoming school holidays, minimum days, field trips, school functions, birthday parties, and any other event you need to be reminded of. Not only will this keep you on task for school events, but it will afford you less chaos by keeping an up-to-date schedule you can refer to.

**Teach your children well.** By planning, initiating, and assisting your children with their homework and class projects in a timely manner, you will indeed teach them the importance of being prompt, efficient, and well-organized. After all, we're raising the multitaskers of the future, aren't we?

**Say "yes".** If you have the time to pull away from your hectic daily schedule, by all means, volunteer in your child's classroom. If you have more than one child, this is the perfect opportunity to give each of your children some precious one-on-one time with you. And what kid doesn't love that? By volunteering, you'll also have the opportunity to observe your child in the classroom setting, get familiar and friendly with other moms, develop a great working relationship with the teacher, and have a whole bunch of fun while you're at it.

**Meet the parents.** The elementary years are pretty formative ones, in which most of our kiddos make lasting friendships. Can you recall your own? It's important, especially in today's world, to know who your kids' friends (and their parents) are, and to become as involved as you possibly can in their social lives. We all know how fast they grow, how quickly they change, and how soon those fabulous opinions—that we have plenty of—will no longer matter. My advice: meet the parents.

**Beware of the 'tude.** Behavioral issues can arise if kiddos are having trouble at school. As a kid, I detested math; it was my mortal enemy. I grew to dislike attending that class—didn't care for my teacher too much either—and had an attitude toward the subject that was less than pleasant. Okay, maybe it was exceedingly horrible. If this is happening with your own child, there are ways to curb it before it becomes a real problem. Meet with their teacher, invest in a tutor, and take the necessary steps to help your child feel less confused and more in control of the concepts.

**Did I mention praying?** If you haven't already noticed, I've mentioned prayer in every single chapter of this book. This isn't an effort on my part to sound redundant; rather, prayer is *the* best tip I can provide when confronted with all of the issues we moms face. Because as parents, it's downright tough sending our little ones off to school, isn't it? It's hard letting go, but this is where the act of prayer becomes so helpful. We need to pray for and with our children each and every day—at the breakfast table, on the way to school, after picking them up, and upon tucking them into their beds each night. Never cease praying, nor underestimate the power of doing so.

Let's face it. We only have a small window of time where our children *choose* to lean on us for support. So let's make sure we're quick to listen and slow to speak, that we embrace them often, praise them just as much, love on them lots, and provide them with the assistance they'll need throughout their school years and beyond. Now is the time to let them know that you've always got their back, no matter what. . . . Well, you and Jesus, that is.

# 9

# DID SOMEONE SAY DIY? THE WANNABE GETS CRAFTY

*"Hand over the glue gun and nobody gets hurt."*

Todays' world—and culture—is totally different from the one I grew up in only a couple of decades ago. How so?

Sewing has become chic.

Homemade clothes are en vogue.

DIY (do it yourself) projects are all the rage.

And craft stores . . . well, craft stores just rule.

Yep. In this day and age, the crafting craze has all but taken over our country, which leaves this Wonder Woman Wannabe weighted down by the creative pressures that get placed squarely upon my shoulders. Do I want to be a crafting genius capable of whipping up a few curtains, a Halloween costume, and maybe a reupholstered chair in my free time? Absolutely. But for me, and maybe a Supermom like you, this is a mission impossible of sorts. Instead, I try my best to scrapbook—although I'm two kids and two years behind on my albums. I take a massive amount of pictures, which I have yet to organize, and once in a while, I muster up the courage to try something new from a tutorial

I've seen online—my attempt at a DIY project I guess. Other than that, while my desire to craft may be there, the time, the energy, and some of the skills required to do so, are not.

Raise your hand if you're with me, girls!

As I see it, there are two types of moms making up our current population: mamas who craft and mamas who don't. Whichever group you belong to, one thing is for certain—crafting in today's society is somewhat of a necessity. After all, our families' memories need to be preserved, and school projects—you know, the ones we described in the previous chapter? Well, those are definitely going to have to be addressed. So what are the non-caped, non-crafty, time-challenged moms supposed to do?

Well, short of paying others to perform these tasks for you, it may just be time to indulge those left-brains a bit more and locate the time needed to spark your creativity.

Did I just hear sighing on your end? Are you in need of a pep talk?

Don't worry, I promise it'll be painless, fairly easy, and you'll love the results. Wanna know more? Keep reading, girls.

## #1: PROJECTS—SEWING, SCISSORS, AND PAPER, OH MY!

There's no denying the fact that as a mom, you will need to brush up on your arts and crafts skills in order to help your children out with one of the many millions of projects they'll likely bring home and seek assistance on. If you're already crafty and have over three thousand pins dealing with creativity—of course I'm referring to Pinterest here—then it looks like you're headed in the right direction. But for those moms who cringe at the thought of combining glue with construction paper, here are some tips that can help when your creative juices flat-out refuse to flow.

**Hit the Internet.** I can't tell you how many crafting sites there are on the Internet—probably because I have yet to make my way through them all. But online assistance is your best resource when taking on a slew of projects with limited skills in your arsenal and no clue as to where you should begin. Need an erupting volcano? Yah, the Internet's got the directions for that. How about plans for making a solar system from scratch? Yep, they've got that, too. Pretty much any type of project that you can think of—or would ever be required to make or supervise—can be located by simply jumping online. Easy squeezy!

**Visit the craft store.** Ahhh, the craft store! Now, I'd be foolish not to mention that these stores (in their monstrosity) can be pretty intimidating, overwhelming, and just plain scary for the population of non-crafting mamas out there. Aisle after aisle of googly eyes, yarn, beads, ribbons, and any other item you can think of are all housed in the confines of these gigantic stores. You name the project, and they've got all of the supplies to assist you in completing it. But have no fear, because help is always near. So, go ahead and pick a project, compile a list of the items you'll need, bring along a friend for moral support, and then head on down to your nearest hobby store—oh, and make sure not to forget your coupons.

**Get resourceful.** When indulging in a new project, especially if it's school-related, you'll want to pinch your pennies as much as feasibly possible. Search for the items you'll need around your house or neighborhood *before* heading to your local craft store. Check with close-by friends or family members in an effort to borrow the essentials your assignment requires, thereby eliminating the need for excess spending. And for those projects that are extremely detailed and involved? Hit up your community, call area businesses, and let them know what you're in need of. Oftentimes you can score a whole bunch of materials for free, just by asking. Hey, it's worth a shot!

**Seek support.** If you despise all things crafty and creative, then by all means, seek the support of your creative friends. Let's be real here, crafting and the like just isn't for everyone, so why not request some support the next time you or one of your children need it? Ignore those underlying pressures to perform, and pursue help instead. More than likely, your friends will be glad to assist you (crafters love a good challenge) while you successfully fend off mounting pressure in the process. Sounds like a win-win situation to me!

**Dealing with the aftermath.** Okay, so let me set the scene here: You've just assisted in building a model volcano that erupts at the touch of a button, oozing what appears to be molten lava, and simulates the activity level of a real, mountainous region. You're proud of your efforts—darn proud, in fact. You, your child, (and possibly the neighbor) worked hard and earned an A for your efforts, but are now faced with the task of figuring out what to do with this ginormous replica forever in your custody. Last time you checked, the Salvation Army wasn't in the market for a three-foot-tall lava-spitting volcano. So, what's a proud parent and equally proud kiddo supposed to do?

Simple: take a picture.

This one act of photographing your child while building their masterpiece will, in fact, save you from storing such a project for an undisclosed period of time. You'll have the memories to remember it by without the inconvenience of accommodating a huge, hissing, messy model on your dining room table for months, or maybe even years, to come. Remember mamas, there's no shame in pitching those projects once they've been graded, just don't forget to document them is all. Yah, taking a picture is a much better idea.

## #2: PHOTOGRAPHY—WAIT, DID SOMEONE SAY "PICTURE?"

They say a picture is worth a thousand words, right? Maybe this is the reason why so many of us moms can't help but become those camera-wielding women everyone's quite familiar with, and possibly annoyed by, at soccer games, ballet recitals, talent shows, and so on. You know—the sort of moms who can't help but snap picture after glorious picture of their children? Whether they're scoring a goal, or picking their nose—nothing is off-limits when women like us are behind the camera.

I'll admit I'm annoying and a bit overzealous when it comes to taking shots of my children. And I'll confess that the moment my kiddos see a flash (no matter whose camera it's coming from), they can't help but strike a pose, widen their smiles, and strain to keep their eyes open. My kids are well aware of the routine and duties required of them once that camera comes out . . . and they've already realized that if mom captures the picture she's looking for on the first try, they won't be subjected to this type of torture any longer than they have to be.

What can I say? I'm a sucker for a great photo opp, but sometimes I take it a bit too far.

How far you ask?

It was just six months ago that my son took a nasty tumble off his bike and made contact with an unforgiving concrete road. My daughter frantically ran to our front door in an effort to tell me what had happened and to get her bleeding (and slightly traumatized) brother the help he needed. So I did what any worried mom might do in that situation: I checked on the status of my son, cared for his wounds, hugged him close . . . and then I grabbed my camera to document this picture-worthy event before it passed me by.

At that exact moment, and once I knew my son was okay, I began to envision the look of the layout I was going to scrapbook, and the types of embellishments I might use to tell this story . . . you know, so he could look back upon those pictures as an adult and be glad I was there, camera in hand.

Hmmm . . . maybe I took this one a little *too* far.

However, most memories that we seek to secure don't involve road rash, knocked-out teeth, or bloody faces. Rather, they're upbeat moments we want to cherish for years to come. So what's the best way to do this? The answer depends upon the amount of energy (and effort) you're willing to exert. It also varies due to your budget and the amount of time you'll be able to dedicate to it. Basically, when it comes to preserving your children's memories, and those of the rest of your family members, there are a number of ways one can go about it.

**Scrapbook albums:** Printed papers, embellishments, various techniques and tools used in the art of scrapbooking all make me giddy with excitement. Gosh, I can't believe I just admitted that. But, if left to my own devices for an undisclosed amount of time, I could easily spend hours, if not days, getting lost in the racks of any designated scrapbooking store. It's a hobby that I enjoy taking part in—one that also happens to be time-consuming, kind of expensive, and habit-forming, too. While this might be *my* personal preference, if you're not a lover of all things crafty by nature, and don't have a lot of time to devote to it, then this method of memory-making may not be for you. Unless you like stickers . . . did I mention how awesome the stickers are? Walls and walls of sticker madness to aid in embellishing those awesome layouts. Check it out for yourself. Oh, yes!

**Photo books:** Never has it been so easy to upload pictures onto the Web, select a few options, and produce a full year of mementos at the click of a button. *Bam!* Instant memories, bound and ready for family members to enjoy and reflect upon for years to come. It's quick, easy, affordable, and pretty painless. And what could be better than that? Take a moment to visit sites such as Shutterfly, Walgreens, Snapfish, or MixBook and check out all of the options available to you when creating these memoirs. You're gonna love the results.

**Photo projects/classes:** Scrapbooking isn't the only hobby that can develop from taking pictures of our little ones. Many moms acquire a passion for photography once they realize how fun capturing pictures of their cute kiddos can be. If this sounds like you, look into programs in your neck of the woods offering instruction on photography, editing, production, and graphic design. Who knows, maybe your love of taking pictures can turn into a profitable business as well. Just sayin'!

**Decorating**: With options just short of a million different uses for your family's photos, taking pictures has never been so much fun. No, really. From free editing services online to creative new ways to have your pictures mounted and displayed, the options are endless when it comes to preserving your precious photos in a creative way. Tap into sites like Pinterest, one of my favorites, or visit your favorite photo-printing sites and discover all that can be done with your precious family photos. Even better, all you have to do is upload your memories, pay the bill, and receive your masterpieces in the mail. That's it . . . crafting, decorating, and creativity made simple. Voila!

## #3: DIY—"I'M SUPPOSED TO DO WHAT MYSELF?"

Yep, I'm going there. I'm venturing into the territory that all non-crafting mamas shudder to think about by discussing all things DIY (as in Do-It-Yourself). It seems these types of in-home projects have achieved a whole new level of popularity in recent years, but as much as I try, I'll wave my white flag and admit that I'm just not made to construct crafts like these. God blessed me with gifts, and gave me a few talents I can claim, but DIY projects? Yah—that wasn't one of them. Don't get me wrong, I could spend all day watching home improvement shows and soaking in all of the DIY greatness, knowing full well that my capabilities in achieving even one of those creations is nil—as in non-existent, not gonna happen. I think I'm what's known as "DIY deficient."

But even if I'm unable to whip up my own backyard deck, make a walkway out of mosaics, or construct a built-in BBQ pit—complete with a fresh, new landscape out in that backyard of mine—maybe I can still figure out a way to break into this crafting craze after all . . . one project at a time. Maybe it's time for *you* to take another look at DIY, too, and attempt to immerse yourself in a project of your own, save some money by doing so, and claim victory in this area once and for all. Never hurts to try, right?

C'mon, it'll be fun. Scout's honor.

And here are some tips to help you on your way.

**Pinterest:** I've mentioned it before, but this one site contains more tutorials for home projects than one would have ever thought possible. We're talking blueprints, plans, instructions, and step-by-step guidelines for pretty much anything you want to achieve in your own home. It's nothing short of amazing, which means even the most challenged DIYer can find a project they can tackle relatively easily. My recommendation? Start small, girls, and grow from there.

**Crafting buddy:** Remember that really crafty friend of yours that helped you out with your kiddo's class project? Well, she's also the gal that can mentor you by teaching you some of the basics to the art of DIYing—if that's even a word. So, go ahead and attack that tufted headboard, get into your sewing groove, and invest some time into accomplishing something, anything, creative. With a crafty friend's guidance, not only will it be fun, it can also be productive. Hey, you never know until you try.

**Class is in session:** Nothing inspires me to engage in a bit of DIYing like those commercials from the big—as in super large—home improvement stores. I watch as pleasantries are exchanged between patron and store employee as they can't help but enjoy the process of learning to grout or lay tile for the first time. They seem happy and uplifted by their frugal achievements. Advertisements like these make me think I can have the same outcome. And why not, I guess? Do yourself a favor, call your local home improvement store and check into the types of classes you can sign up for. It's DIY made easy, and cheap, girls. See? I told you it would be painless!

Now, if you're a crafting whiz and resident genius in all things creative, then this chapter was probably old news to you. But for the rest of the mommy population that possibly struggles with all things artsy, I hope the advice within provided some reassurance and encouragement that no matter your skill level, you too can accomplish craftiness . . . one project at a time.

# SECTION II

# THE WONDER WOMAN WANNABE RUNS A HOUSEHOLD

10

# WONDER WOMAN INVESTS IN A CROCKPOT: MOONLIGHTING AS A MEAL PLANNER

*"So whether you eat or drink or whatever you do, do all to the glory of God."*

**—1 Corinthians 10:31**

I love food.

I love to eat food.

But when it comes to cooking food? Well, let's just say it's not my *thang*.

But it's not as if I haven't tried. In fact, in the past ten plus years I've been a married gal, I've established quite a collection of cookbooks. More than I can count. I've invested in numerous gadgets, trinkets, and devices to help make the time spent in my kitchen easier—on me that is. I've even researched blogs and websites in an attempt to bring out my inner chef—you know, the one that's supposedly residing within. But alas, all efforts seemed to have been in vain. After falling short of the culinary wizardry I've desired, secretly, all these years, it has become blatantly apparent that not only am I *no* Wonder Woman, but I'm definitely *no* Julia Child, either.

So, what's a mom in my situation to do?

Well, short of having our own, personal chef to figure out those nightly struggles of "what's for dinner," the answer can basically be summed up into two words: meal preparation.

Now, I'm guessing that most of you ladies have heard of meal planning, right? While this concept certainly may not be groundbreaking information to the maternal population, it can be a bit of a struggle for some of us gals to implement. Initially, the mere thought of planning my meals weeks in advance was enough to cause a slight meltdown. I for one was not necessarily searching for another task to add to my ever-growing, and quite exhausting list of to-dos. But after years of fixing concoctions that failed to resonate with my family members—as indicated by the uneaten residual left on their plates—I had grown desperate and weary from the battle that raged between me and my kitchen, night after night. I had no other choice but to finally incorporate a bi-weekly meal plan of my own.

And I'm *so* glad I did. Meal planning has become a life-saver.

By following the super simple tips I'm about to divulge, and at the risk of sounding like a really bad infomercial here, you'll never have had dinner plans so easy, budget-friendly, and—yep, you guessed it—stress-free. You don't have to be a gourmet chef in order to excel at or successfully execute the concept of meal planning either.

So, are you ready to make dinner more about spending time with our sweet families, and appreciating the bounty in front of us, and less about worrying how it's going to get there? Let's do this, ladies.

## MEAL PLANNING: THE 4-1-1

*"I am not a glutton—I am an explorer of food."*

**—Erma Bombeck**

Prior to my meal planning endeavors, my cooking routine consisted of a boring rotation of dinners usually prepared by Stouffer's or some other brand of frozen food that I could reheat and feed to my family with little to no effort at all. It was only on the rare occasion, such as holidays or when I got the inkling—which wasn't all that often due to the schedule I was keeping—that I could devote any sort of time and energy to creating delicious meals. Hey, I may not have been the greatest cook, but when given the time to do so, I found joy in planning and preparing small feasts for my family.

But when it came to doing this on a daily basis? Eh, maybe not so much.

Like most busy moms, the time that I would normally dedicate to preparing nightly meals became quickly consumed by hauling kiddos back and forth to various functions and activities, leaving little to no room in my agenda to worry about fixing dinner. I'll confess that my lack of efficient planning also led to numerous and pretty consistent visits to the drive-thru, which negated any attempt of trying to feed my kids a healthy, balanced diet. For me, there just had to be a better way to provide my children with quick, nutritious meals they'd actually enjoy eating (and that wouldn't cause me undue angst in preparing them).

Sound familiar? Bring on the meal planning!

It seems as though there are a lot of choices to make when it comes to putting edible food on the table each night, doesn't it? But rest assured; meal planning is nothing more than picking out recipes, buying ingredients, and then assembling those items together to form an actual meal. Sounds easy enough, right? Here are the tips to help you launch a super successful, convenient, and delicious meal plan—all while saving your sweet sanity:

**Decision time**: The first decision you'll have to make as a meal-planning mama, is how far in advance you want to set up your meal calendar. A week? Two weeks? A month? Three years? I'm kidding, of course. Fortunately, there is no wrong way of doing this . . . just as long as you *do* it! Consider what will work best for you and your family's needs and make your decision accordingly.

**All about the options**: There's a method to this meal-planning madness, which means you'll need to make a choice as to how involved you want to be when organizing your dinnertime agenda. Basically, you just need to figure out what's going to work for you, your schedule, and your family. For instance, would you prefer to use your own recipes and organize your suppertime schedule all on your own? Would you rather use a Web site that specializes in planning your meals for you?

How about that freezer of yours? Would you rather make a whole bunch of meals and then use that thing to store them? Or, would you opt to pay for a service that will cook and deliver your food right to your doorstep? Wow! Doesn't that sound nice? Need more information? Here's a better description of some of these options.

### *The "old-school, my-recipes-rock, DIY" meal-planning mama*

If you've got an arsenal of family recipes just waiting to be prepared, then by all means, organize those recipes in calendar form, purchase your ingredients, and get cooking. By opting for this DIY version of meal strategizing, you are basically at the helm of selecting items and dinners that your family will enjoy devouring. Whether it's using your own personal resources or those found online (such as informative blogs, cooking sites, magazines, etc.), DIY meal planning can be fun, satisfying and delicious . . . and you don't have to be an expert in the kitchen to be successful at it. *Bonus!*

### *The "techno-savvy, non-traditionalist" meal-planning mama*

Armed with your Wi-Fi and PC, a whole new world of meal-making opportunities can be at your fingertips. Yes, that sounded completely cheesy. But thanks to the Internet, meal planning has become techno-friendly and extremely easy to implement into our hectic schedules. By subscribing to online Web sites geared specifically toward meal plan organization—emeals.com, plantoeat.com, and cookingplanit.com, just to name a few—not only will you be able to select the types of foods you want to ingest, but you'll also be in control of modifying the meals based on the dietary needs of your family. For a small monthly fee, a customized meal calendar will be devised and organized based on the dietary requirements you select. Other than printing off your lists and venturing to the store to gather your items, there's really no other work involved . . . well, except for actually preparing the meal itself, of course. So, whether you want lower-calorie menu items or prefer a strictly vegetarian diet, these sites provide extremely convenient options. Just type in your requests and *poof!*, your meal plan and selected recipes are ready to be printed and made. So savvy!

### *The "freeze-it-and-leave-it" meal-planning mama*

Talk about a stress reliever! It turns out that the really cold rectangular box connected to the fridge is pretty handy when used properly. Other than storing waffles, meat, and veggies, it can also house pre-made meals that can be reheated and served at dinnertime. Yep, by preparing a week's worth of meals in advance, there's no stress and nothing to fret over during the week. And let's be honest here, it's pretty reassuring, after a long day of shuttling kids to and fro, to know that dinner is already prepared and just one step away from being on my family's plates.

### *The "don't-bug-me, money-is-not-an-issue" meal-planning mama*

If you don't want to be bothered with the planning, cooking, or purchasing aspects of meal planning—then designer food service facilities may be more your speed. They literally decide every aspect of your meal, cook it, and deliver it for a slightly outrageous fee. This is one step away from having your own personal chef, and if you can afford it, then by all means, go for it. *Ooh la la!*

So what's next? Well, after you've looked through your options and selected the type of meal planning that will work best for your brood—whether using your own recipes or Web sites and magazine recipes—now's the time to start constructing your meal calendar (unless of course you've selected option number four as mentioned above). Keep in mind that when choosing meals, you'll want to look at total prep and cooking times for each one. No matter how good a dinner may look, if the preparation is too lengthy, and fairly involved, it's probably not the best choice for a busy weeknight. Rather, save something that fabulous for when you have more time . . . like maybe on the weekend, perhaps.

Oh, and what's even better than finding recipes on your own? That would be enlisting the help of your kids! Hey, our children love being involved in the process of making decisions—no matter what they are. Having them select a meal or two of their own and assist in making it can also provide some great bonding between mom and child. Besides, with all the time we're now saving by implementing meal preparation into our schedules, we'll be able to have more moments with the ones who need it most—our babies. Get your kids involved with meal prep and they may just scarf all of their dinner down the next time their selected meal is made. Wouldn't that be nice?

Now that you've been briefed on the types of meal plans out there—and have hopefully selected the right plan for your needs—it's time to take the next steps. Yep. It's time to make your list, check it twice—if need be—and start shopping, girls.

**She's making a list**: Your meals are scheduled and your calendar is complete. Looks like it's time to furnish yourself with a list of ingredients you'll need to prepare all the deliciousness you just spent time mapping out. Write 'em down or plug 'em into your phone, put 'em in your purse, and get ready to get some groceries, girls.

**Shoppin' time**: Now, we'll get into the couponing craze a little bit later in this book, but for now, equip yourself with your list, whatever coupons you might have, and go get your food. Don't be surprised at the time of checkout if your bill is actually lower—yes, *lower!*—than before you began your meal planning endeavors. This is just another bonus feature to planning your dinners in advance . . . you get to save money in the process. See, it does pay off!

**Got doubts?** Hey, if you're new to this and still feeling slightly overwhelmed with the information provided, you may just need a little more instruction on how it all works. Thankfully, there are numerous Web sites offering their services (and free information) on how to do this meal planning thing just right. Just hit the Internet for even more fabulous tips.

So what do you think? Sounds easy enough, right? Well, here's the thing: up until this point, I have not yet shared with you the one, best-kept secret of modern-day meal planning that no Wonder Woman Wannabe should ever be without. We're talking about a revolutionary product ideal for preparing meals . . . a device that's probably sitting right there in your home (possibly behind the deep fryer and amongst the other products lost in your kitchen cabinet contraption graveyard), just waiting to be used. It's a machine so revolutionary I believe it should be considered a culinary miracle of sorts.

Yes, ladies . . . I'm talking about your Crock-Pot.

## THE WANNABE INVESTS IN A CROCK-POT.

> *"Food cooks all day while the cook's away. . . .*
> *It's like having your own cook."*
>
> **—Crock-Pot commercial, 1974**

Honestly, who invented this fabulous gadget and then labeled it with the less than appetizing (and slightly icky) name of "Crock-Pot"?? I mean, C-r-o-c-k-P-o-t? As in a pot of crock? Whatever the case, this invention is one huge blessing of a cooking machine indeed . . . especially for us modern-day moms on the go.

The Crock-Pot is also known as a "slow-cooker" and was probably the one item you deemed truly unnecessary and potentially useless when your mother made you register for it as a wedding gift. Fast forward to the present-day, and you may be a gal unwilling to ever part with this masterpiece of a machine. After all, we are moms in need of convenience and the Crock-Pot (ugh, that name!) embodies the very essence of this principle like no other culinary aid we possess.

Admittedly, I wasn't always the slow-cooking fanatic that I am today. Unaware of the superpowers this product possessed, I let that sweet machine sit for *years!* in the back of my kitchen cabinet, collecting dust. I honestly had no clue as to its time-saving capabilities or the delicious dinners it could have provided my family, with little-to-no effort on my part.

I'll confess that I was pretty skeptical of such a device at first. I mean, anything that is plugged into an electrical outlet of your home and cooks food for roughly ten hours straight should technically burn your house down. But not this machine. Nope, not the pot of crock. Amazingly enough, all one needs to do is load this baby up with the desired ingredients, turn it on, and then return home later to gobble up its goodness. It is just that simple. And, using a slow-cooker as your preferred method of cooking is nothing short of brilliant, if you ask me. Think about it: our families are growing, our schedules are crazy, and oftentimes we're being tugged in all different directions, whether we want to be or not. The slow cooker is a great way of preparing food that will accommodate all of your family's scheduling needs, while ensuring a hot, delicious dinner each and every time. Yep, just call me the official endorser of this machine.

So, if you're a mom who's got a PTA board meeting at six in the evening but has a hubby and kids who won't arrive home until eight, you can rest assured knowing that your slow cooker will provide them with a hot, home-cooked meal, no matter what time they finally get around to eating it. No microwaves needed and only minimal effort required on the part of mom.

Can I get an "amen"?

Now, if you haven't invested in a Crock-Pot—or currently have yours still boxed in storage after you received it for a wedding present years ago—go get it and start putting that thing to good use. In fact, one of the best things you can do to help jump-start your slow-cooking routine is to use your favorite search engine on the Internet to check out what other moms are making, what recipes they like the best, and what meals fit nicely into your grocery budget. I think you may be pleasantly surprised by what this one piece of kitchen machinery can do for your meal planning, budget, and overall stress level.

## USING YOUR CROCKPOT: EASY AS 1-2-3!

Want to know how you can get started using your Crock-Pot right now? It is so unbelievably easy that if you haven't yet familiarized yourself with this heavenly hot pot, you'll be singing its praises very soon. Here's what to do:

1. Dig that Crock-Pot out of the pantry, box, or cupboard you currently hide it in.
2. Dust it off, or maybe even wash it.
3. Visit the Internet and perform an online search for all blogs and sites offering slow cooker meal plans and recipes. I love the site that starts with a "P" and ends with "interest."
4. Pick out the meals you want to try and then purchase the necessary ingredients.
5. Choose one day, like Sunday after church, to combine the ingredients needed for each meal into a freezer-safe bag for each night of the week.
6. Place each meal-in-a-bag into the freezer. Make sure it is labeled and dated.
7. Each morning, select a bag out of the freezer, unload the contents into your slow-cooking magic machine, push the button, and cover.
8. If not interested in steps 5–7, gather your ingredients early in the day, dump them into your Crock-Pot, and hit the "start" button.
9. Sit back, flex a muscle or two, and ponder how much you rock and how in-control of dinnertime you are. *Pow!*

Oh, and keep in mind that a slow cooker can be used for much more than just dinners. There are recipes also geared for some seriously yummy breakfast items, desserts, and tasty appetizers, too. Gosh, I love me a Crock-Pot. It seriously does make life—as far as our cooking duties are concerned—a whole, heck-of-a-lot easier. So, how about it girls? Get out your recipes or get online, and get ready to make dinnertime easy again. The slow cooker: it's just not for collecting dust anymore.

11

# THE WANNABE CLEANS THE BATHROOM—AND DOES THE DISHES, TOO

*"I'm not going to vacuum 'til Sears makes one you can ride on."*

**—Roseanne Barr**

So let me get this straight: not only are we supposed to feed our families, care for their needs, transport them to and fro, run errands, and do laundry, but we're also the gals in charge of scrubbing toilets, cleaning windows, doing dishes, and ensuring that our homes don't become the next dwellings featured on a television show about hoarding.

And we don't get paid for this?

Am I missing something here?

Let me be honest and up front by first stating that I *detest* housework—we're talking with a capital D, ladies. The mere thought of it makes me twitch, convulse, and on really bad days can even send me into a full-fledged adult temper tantrum—as in an episode involving kicking, screaming, gnashing of teeth, stomping of feet, and maybe even an out-of-body experience or two.

Admittedly, I have a horrible attitude when it comes to completing my chores, and I seriously struggle with finding joy in any of them. Call me crazy, but I for one do not take pleasure in washing fecal residue from a porcelain bowl . . . or four. Nor do I particularly love scouring my shower door in an effort to try and see through it once in a while. And this might sound really off the wall, but picking up my dog's poop from the backyard each and every day is just not a "duty" I want to partake in. I loathe dog poop. Heck, I loathe poop of any kind.

Now, I think I can speak for a lot of us moms when I state that the motivation needed to effectively and routinely clean our homes is lacking from time to time—or all of the time in my case. With three beautiful children who continually conspire against me to create domestic anarchy, the task of cleaning is seemingly a never-ending gig (and I mentioned I don't get paid, right? No allowance, no chocolate, nada). This said task leaves me feeling more like a residential cleaning service and less like the mommy God designed me to be. Day after day, I'm confronted by crumbs of food on my floor, smudges on my windows, footprints on my walls, and toothpaste on my mirrors—it's not a pretty scene, to say the least.

And what about my kids you ask? Where are they in all of this? They're too busy having fun and loving life to bother worrying about whether they spilled a whole gallon of milk on the floor, or if the cat just used the new couch as a scratching post. Cleaning in general is not on their radar. Unfortunately, most of the time, it's all I can concentrate on.

But I'm a mom, and what's more, I'm a Christian mom who's in need of some serious grace—and one huge attitude adjustment—when it comes to tackling this grueling task. Having a horrible disposition toward my to-do list is not the aura I want to exude, nor is it the type of example I want to set for my young children. Rather, I need to be thankful that I have a home to clean. I need to feel blessed that I have indoor plumbing and don't have to retreat outside in order to take care of business. And each time I pick up a doggy nugget (or ten), I must remind myself to have an attitude of gratitude ... no matter how unpleasant or smelly the task in front of me might be. At times this can be hard, because as moms it seems as though disorderly chaos tends to follow us everywhere, consuming us all too often and way too much. It can feel as if our homes are literally closing in around us, and the total disarray—that we didn't create in the first place—may in fact devour us whole. It's at this point that frustration and anxiety creep in and a major mommy meltdown is only minutes—if not seconds—away. Rather than focusing on the blessings that surround us, we're stuck fretting over the unkempt state they're in.

All this and it's not even nine o'clock in the morning yet.

Well, whether we created the clutter or not, more than likely, we're the gals in charge of cleaning it up. We are the captains of such chaos, the domestic directors in charge . . . we're the girls running the joint. Should our homes really be a source of so much stress or a dwelling that holds us captive by our lack of desire to clean it? Of course not. "Home" should be so much more than the place where we happen to launder, change sheets, or clean windows. It's not just where our mops are stored or dust collects. Our homes are meant to serve as safe havens for our families, places where lasting memories are made, and the locations where we live out our lives.

"Home is where your story begins." And if that's the case—and I do believe it is—it looks like it's time to get a cleaning schedule that will succeed in reducing our labor, minimize our angst toward this task, and allow us to spend more time with our precious families, instead.

Sounds good, right? Keep reading, girls.

## MINDING THE MESS AND CLEANING IT UP

I think we've already uncovered the fact that motherhood can get rather messy. I'm certain that we're all well aware of how much time is spent each day cleaning up after our children. For me, it feels like every waking minute. *Every.* Waking. Minute. But why the heck should we focus any more attention on housework when we can devote that time toward our family and friends, instead? Yep, when it comes to this cleaning stuff, maybe we just need to push the inner Wonder Woman—the one we're trying to channel—aside and pull out a pair of big, ole blinders, instead. I for one need to ignore the dust bunnies, embrace the smudges, and forget about those annoying crumbs covering my floor. I mean, my number one goal in raising my kids is to spend time enjoying them, not cooped up in the bathroom with a can of disinfectant in one hand and a toilet bowl brush in the other. This girl—yes, me!—wants to be having more fun with the family God gave her, not struggling to uphold her Supermom façade. So, how does a woman achieve said feat without feeling overwhelmed and slightly plagued by the clutter surrounding her? The answer may be simpler than you think.

**Gettin' real.** Isn't it slightly unrealistic for us moms to expect our homes to remain immaculate when we have destructive little munchkins currently residing in them? We ladies need to get honest about our expectations for our homes, and I'll start by publicly professing that the inside of my house may never . . . strike that . . . *will* never be featured in nor resemble something out of a magazine. In fact, after recently peeling back the cushions to my living room couch, it appears I have additional evidence as to why: fragments of stale potato chips, one of Elmo's long-lost eyeballs (seriously), video games (expensive ones at that), a bouncy ball, some spare change, and poor Barbie's misplaced espadrille—who knows how long that girl had been limping around without her designer shoe.

Rather than constantly focusing on the disorderly state of my home, I need to get real in setting out to achieve rational housework objectives instead. I've got to think about the bigger picture here and ditch the unrealistic expectations that disfigure my thoughts on a daily basis. I need to get my issues with cleaning under control once and for all . . . before I end up like Martha (and I don't mean Martha Stewart here).

You remember the biblical story of Mary and Martha and the day Jesus came to visit them, right? Well, whether or not you're familiar with this age-old account—and first documented case of OCD—allow me to provide you with a point of reference . . . and a lesson in humility.

Mary and Martha were two sisters notified one day that Jesus—*Jesus!*—might be in their neck of the woods, and may be inclined to pay them both a visit. Beyond excited at the mention of such news—and who wouldn't be, really?—Mary immediately began to prepare for her encounter with the Christ, while Martha did what any of us modern-day mamas would do and ran for her dust rag and broom instead. It appeared that Martha was quite aware there wouldn't be a second chance to make a first impression on the Son of God, and became all-too-consumed with checking off the items on her biblical to-do list. So consumed, in fact, that she missed out on her chance to hang out with Jesus. You know—Jesus: the King of Kings, the Great I Am, the Wonderful Counselor, the Savior Himself? Yep, Martha was so distracted by her household duties that she passed up the one opportunity to sit down and spend time face-to-face with her Savior.

*Whoa!* And I thought my OCD was bad.

However, Mary's story was much, much different than her sister's. Mary was a gal who had it all figured out. When Jesus came around, she took time to tend to Him, sat down with Him, washed His feet and took in His presence. She wasn't about to let a few trivial household chores distract from her time with the Great I Am.

Mary had it together. Martha on the other hand? That girl was struggling.

I mean, did she honestly think that Jesus would have walked into her home, become disgusted by the amount of dust on her clay pots, and then bolt out the door in an effort to find a dwelling that didn't house a bunch of slobs? Not likely. But at the time, in Martha's mind, housework and chores were all she could focus on. The girl just couldn't help herself.

Sound familiar?

As easy as it might be for us to pass judgment on Martha, chances are, we might have behaved the same way. I can only hope I would be wise enough not to pass up on the opportunity to meet with Jesus Christ. In my mind, I would drop my mop in a heartbeat for that. But knowing my Martha-like tendencies, I'm not so sure I would have in the moment. You see, I tend to worry way too much about the state of my house rather than the amount of quality time I'm spending with my sweet family. Sad, I know.

Martha was in dire need of a lesson in keeping it real, wasn't she? Guess what? Many of us moms, me included, are in need of the exact same thing.

So, let's keep this in mind, girls, when we become consumed with the state of our homes. Let the image of Martha running around her house, ignoring Jesus, remind us all that we must try to refrain from becoming overwhelmed by such issues. We can be neat but we don't necessarily have to be neat-freaks. See the difference? Let's keep it real, shall we?

**Gettin' on a schedule.** Open. Shut. Open. Shut. As I stumble upon yet another mess in my home, my immediate thought is to close my eyes and pray that, upon reopening them, the clutter before me will have magically disappeared. As you might have guessed, divine intervention doesn't exactly work this way—no matter how much I pray. And so I must resort to other, more creative methods of cleaning my home.

Enter brilliant idea number two, and the slightly maniacal motions made as I begin snapping my fingers in the hopes that the sounds my appendages produce will result in a chore-whispering effect over my entire home. It worked for Mary Poppins, right? *Snap!* And those untidy beds of mine are suddenly made tidy. The toys strewn all over the floor willingly make their way into storage bins, all while I sing a joyful song, and watch as my house is cleaned right in front of my very eyes—with no effort on my part whatsoever . . . aside from snapping my fingers that is. Yah . . . like that's about to happen either! The only thing this method achieves is looking like a crazed housewife with a snapping issue, rather than a gal just trying to will her home into a more perfect state. Imagine that.

All joking aside though, after becoming a mom, I was in need of figuring out a way to keep my house clean, manage those messes, save my sanity, ditch my Martha tendencies, and also make room for more family time. I needed a real plan for how to deal with my contagious clutter, in a timely manner, without allowing it to drive me crazy in the process. Like you, I was a mom in need of a quick, yet painless way to clean my home. Would professional reinforcements (a.k.a. housekeepers) help? Absolutely. But for me and perhaps for you as well, they just weren't an option I could financially incorporate into our household budget. Don't get me wrong, I've dreamt of a sparkling clean, disinfected house that required absolutely no participation on my part whatsoever. But in reality, if any cleaning was going to take place, it was going to be up to me to take care of it. This is where a schedule came in to play, complete with a list of household chores, an effective time frame to accomplish them, and the assistance of my children in order to execute them. With only thirty minutes (per day) devoted to housework, this cleaning fiasco is about to get fun . . . well, under control anyway.

Wait! Did you read what I just wrote, girls? A clean home in only thirty minutes! Yes, thirty minutes is all you will need per day to complete those pesky house chores around your home. Thirty minutes and you are done . . . as in D-O-N-E! Just think about this for a moment because half an hour is totally doable, right? Here's how.

## MAKE A LIST (YOU DON'T HAVE TO CHECK IT TWICE)

Effective cleaning is about devising a customized schedule of your household needs and personal preferences. You have to ask yourself what matters most to you, as far as cleanliness goes? Vacuumed carpets? Spotless mirrors and windows? Debris-free hardwood floors? By configuring a tailored list, based on your desires, you can divvy up your chores throughout the week and make your household duties doable. I think I feel the stress lifting off of your shoulders already, and a huge sigh of relief on your end. Furthermore, your housework should be broken down into two different areas: chores performed daily, and those completed once a week. Remember: the goal is to spend no more than thirty minutes a day —*woo hoo!*—designated to your household chores. Here's an example of just one sanity-saving schedule:

### *The Thirty-Minutes-per-Day, Weekly Sanity-Saving Schedule*

**Monday:** Dust entire house, including all knick-knacks, furniture, baseboards, window treatments, and fans. (20 minutes)
**Tuesday:** Pick a bathroom or two and clean thoroughly, including shower, tub, floors, mirrors, and toilet. (20–30 minutes)
**Wednesday:** Clean all windows, mirrors, and television sets. Wipe down walls. Change sheets. (30 minutes)
**Thursday:** Mop all floors, and vacuum. (30 minutes)
**Friday:** Pick another bathroom or two: just depends on how many you have. (20–30 minutes)
**Saturday:** Small projects, minor organizing, get rid of the junk mail. (20–30 minutes)

### *Daily Chore List*

- ★ Clean off kitchen countertops, stove, and microwave oven. (10 minutes)
- ★ One load of laundry—or two if you're feeling really crazy. (20 minutes)
- ★ Toy pick-up. (10 minutes)
- ★ Sweep floors. (5 minutes)
- ★ Emptying/loading dishwasher. (10 minutes)
- ★ Trash. (5 minutes)
- ★ Make beds, if so inclined. (10 minutes)

Obviously, this type of list can be changed based upon your personal preferences. It's completely customizable. So head on over to your computer, pull up a spreadsheet, and start making your own list of to-dos to be completed in a fraction of the time it once took doing them all in one day—or every day for us Wonder Woman Wannabes. Easy enough, right? *Ka-pow!*

## GET HELP

I'm quite aware of what you're probably thinking at this point. After browsing through the above schedule, and then totaling the suggested sum of minutes on the list of chores described, you're deliberating where I got my numbers from, and might be pondering if I had problems passing second grade math. My figures just don't add up. They actually surpass the half-hour mark by a decent amount of time, don't they?

This was intentional.

The schedule of tasks shown above wasn't devised to factor in only one participant. Nope, this list was created with the idea that you will become a contributing member to a *team* of housecleaners—inclusive of those cute kids who refer to you as "mom"—as opposed to flying solo. Together with your children, and maybe even your spouse as well, you can accomplish these jobs with ease and officially say "good-bye!" to the stresses that cleaning a home can bring.

Seems pretty simple if I do say so myself, but if you're anything like me—the Wonder Woman Wannabe—at this point you might be struggling with one major issue: perfectionism. For moms like us, we find it much harder to assign chores to our children because we spend most of our time fretting over the outcome of their efforts. I'll even confess that I've been guilty of pushing my children away from participating in family chores because I found it easier to complete them on my own. Hey, issues with perfectionism can be hard to let go of, but we have to realize that if our children are going to learn the importance of responsibility and contributing to a family unit, then by all means, we must provide them with the opportunity and instruction on how to do so.

Are they going to fold towels the way we prefer? I doubt it.

Are their beds going to be made perfectly each and every time? Probably not.

Would their dish-washing abilities pass inspection at a local restaurant? My guess is, no. At least not at first. But they will never know how well they can do if they're not given the chance to at least try. Give your children the opportunity to embrace responsibility, and lighten your workload at the same time. You may just be surprised.

## "BUT MY KIDS ARE TOO YOUNG FOR CHORES . . ."

*"It is not what you do for your children,*
*but what you have taught them to do for themselves*
*that will make them successful human beings."*

**—Ann Landers**

I used to live under this false pretense, too. I once believed that my children shouldn't have any chores until they reached the age of at least eight or so. I just didn't feel they could handle them . . . that, and I was slightly anal retentive at the time. I finally learned that kids—we're talking toddlers all the way up to teenagers—should in fact participate by assuming age-specific responsibilities within the home. Now, I'm not suggesting that you turn your two-year-old loose with the lawn mower or anything like that, but by following the guidelines listed below, here are just a few examples of the types of chores you can expect from your children based upon their ages.

### *Age-Appropriate Chores for Children*

**Toddler** (ages 2–4)

- ☆ Picking up & putting away toys, clothes, and other items
- ☆ Dusting
- ☆ Taking out the trash
- ☆ Restocking the toilet paper
- ☆ Feeding their pets

**Preschooler** (ages 4–5)

- ☆ All toddler chores
- ☆ Loading (and possibly emptying) the dishwasher (under supervision)
- ☆ Helping with getting the mail
- ☆ Putting groceries away
- ☆ Cleaning the windows
- ☆ Basic folding (think socks, underwear, etc.)
- ☆ Weeding and gardening (with supervision)

**Elementary** (ages 6–11)

- ☆ All toddler and preschool chores
- ☆ Wiping down all major surfaces
- ☆ Washing/drying dishes
- ☆ Sweeping
- ☆ Vacuuming
- ☆ Cleaning small appliances (microwave)
- ☆ Mopping floors

- ✰ Making their beds
- ✰ Making simple meals, side dishes, desserts, etc.

**Middle School** (ages 12–14)

- ✰ All previous chores
- ✰ Mowing the lawn (under supervision)
- ✰ Washing/drying of their own clothes
- ✰ Cleaning out fridge/freezer
- ✰ Babysitting (closer to the age of fourteen is best)
- ✰ Supervising siblings' chores (younger, of course)

**High School** (15–18)

- ✰ Responsibilities galore. Anything an adult can do, this age group should be able to help out with, as well.

So, there you have it, moms. By enlisting the help of our kids, husbands, parents, neighbors, or any other passers-by off the street if they're willing to commit, we can ditch the need for perfectionism and incorporate a "team" mentality within our homes. Life with children is going to be fairly messy most of the time, but in order to survive it, we must stay calm, learn to let go, seek prayer for those anxious moments we'll likely endure, and incorporate the attitude of Mary . . . not Martha.

## A FEW BONUS TIPS

*Psst.* . . . Want some additional tips to help you throughout your cleaning endeavors? Implement these savvy time-savers to your cleaning regimen as well.

**Get organized.** Organize your cleaning products by having a central location for all of your items. Got a two- (or three-) story home? Purchase your favorite cleaning products and create a cleaning station for each floor of your home. As mentioned earlier, this will save a lot of time and will reduce frustration as well. Amen to that!

**Brush up.** Got more than one bathroom? Then invest in a toilet cleaning brush for each one of your lavatories. The last thing you want to do is carry remnants of fecal residue (and a dripping toilet wand) around your freshly cleaned home. "*Ew!*" Make that "*Double Ew!*"

**Bust the boredom.** Avoid the monotony associated with cleaning. Even though we've reduced your housework to just a half hour per day, you can eliminate the boredom associated with it by grabbing your iPod or other music-producing device and gettin' your groove on. Try producing your own housecleaning playlist to help make the time spent doing chores go by just a little bit faster. Warning: implement dance moves at your own risk, and always remember to stretch prior to.

**Incorporate lists, and lots of them.** Help keep your family on track by posting cleaning schedules and chore assignments in your home. Hey, nothing screams efficiency like breaking down your family's to-do list by day, week, and month, and then displaying it for all family members to see, and achieve. Take care of your home better, together.

**Pray!** By praying for your children or just having a chat with God while performing your chores, it can help lighten your mood and take the negative thoughts associated with housework away. Try it and see. It works!

# 12

# THE WANNABE VS. THE WASHING MACHINE

*"Despite what anyone may think (or try to coax themselves into believing), the laundry pile is not loads of fun . . . it's loads of work."*

**—The Wannabe**

So here we are again, discussing in yet another chapter of this book how to deal with our pesky housework in the most efficient way possible. Thus far, we've figured out how to stock our cars, plan meals, schedule chores, maintain our homes, and now? Well, now we're going to discuss the one duty that we just can't ignore . . . no matter how hard we try. A chore that's so massive, I've dedicated a whole chapter to it specifically.

It's time to have a serious chat about the laundry.

*Ugh!* The laundry!

Gosh, every time I hear that word uttered, the demeanor of my body instantly undergoes a metamorphosis of sorts. My shoulders slouch, my mouth veers downward, and a sullen expression graces my face, as I hesitantly trudge to the back of my home to begin another load of wash. It is there, in the cave of clothes that I must mercilessly attend to—pile after pile of soiled apparel. This one task has me longing for the days when washing clothes was a burden my mother once lovingly embraced, not me. I get lost in thought as I journey into those good ol' memories of laundry-free living.

You see, even though I've been washing clothes my entire adult life, it wasn't until I turned eighteen and was a fresh face on my college campus that I was abruptly introduced to the world of laundering full-time, as in doing it all on my own. There was no contact, nor was there any sort of relationship between the washer, the dryer, and little old me prior to this major event. I knew those big white boxes cleaned my clothes, but I certainly had no idea how . . . nor did I have any interest in ever finding out.

Yes, I was spoiled, but at the time I never even realized it. But I do now.

Fast forward fifteen years or so, and I'm a woman still hoping that each night my mom will somehow relieve me from my laundry duties once again. Does she live two thousand miles away? Yes, yes she does. Are my thoughts silly and bordering on wildly illogical? Yes, yes they are. (But Mom, if you're reading this and miss the days of old where my heaps of clothes once consumed *you*, by all means call me and we can work something out.)

Somehow, I don't think my phone will be ringing anytime soon.

Looks like I'm still on my own with this one, but I guess I shouldn't grumble, huh?

## NO ROOM TO COMPLAIN

It's very easy for us to look at the tasks in front of us and become overwhelmed, exasperated, and in need of a major venting session. We take comfort in complaining about the work we must endure, not realizing that the more we grumble, the further we stray from God's desires for us. As I've mentioned before, this type of attitude helps no one, especially me, and is just evidence that the "horned one"—a.k.a. he who must not be named but resides down below in a really hot inferno—is succeeding in skewing my attitude and disposition and ridding me of my ability to seek joy in all situations. Besides, compared to yesteryear and laundering duties of old, I must declare that we modern-day mamas have it much easier than our female lineage from long ago.

> *"Do everything without complaining or arguing, so that you may become blameless and pure, children of God without fault in a crooked and depraved generation, in which you shine like stars in the universe."*
>
> **—Philippians 2:14–15**

Not sure what I'm referring to? Maybe it's time for a history lesson of sorts.

Way back in the day, in a much simpler time, washing one's clothes was not only time-consuming, but a real pain in the posterior—much more so than today. As you already know, there was no such thing as high-efficiency washers and dryers or stain-fighting cleaning products available at the nearest grocery store. There were no softening agents or anti-static sheets, either. Our poor foremothers were forced to use something called a washboard along with some unsanitary water from their well (or local stream) in order to "clean" our oh-so-stinky forefathers' garments.

Well, that doesn't sound like fun, now does it?

When washing machines finally came around—and dryers weren't—laundering still remained a time-consuming, labor-intensive task, and all drying of clothes took place on a clothesline. And get this, way back when, our grandmothers and great-grandmothers *ironed.* A lot. As in every day and pretty much everything they washed. I actually learned that my own grandmother opted to iron my grandfather's underwear in addition to every other piece of clothing she labored over.

Underwear!

It sounds to me like I have absolutely no room to complain. Which I already knew well before I lodged the complaint in the first place. I mean, these days, all we have to do is throw in some clothes, some chemicals, select a setting on our convenient machines, and we're done . . . well, with the washing and drying aspect at least. When it comes to folding clothes and putting them away, that's another issue entirely. But that's where this chapter is going to come in handy. Like every other chore we moms partake in, we need to face it, embrace it, and make sure that the simple act of cleaning clothes will not consume our days—and quite possibly our nights, too.

But before we go any further, let me first divulge that I am not now, nor will I ever be, an expert in laundering apparel. I am not the gal capable of assisting you with the ins and outs of laundering itself. Furthermore, it's pretty safe to say that this chapter will not offer tips on how to remove set-in stains or explain the art of getting your whites whiter than, well, white; nor will it provide detailed instructions on how to make your own, homemade laundry detergent. Rather, this portion of the book has been set aside to instruct you on how to organize an efficient laundering schedule and provide you with the tips you'll need to get your clothes washed, dried, folded, and put away in record time. All so that you can move on with your day and away from that washing machine. And I, for one, am totally on board with that.

## GET ORGANIZED: SETTING UP A SCHEDULE

All right, let's get down to business and begin devising a laundry schedule that's functional for you and your family's needs. Another schedule you ask? This may be the point where your eyes have rolled to the back of your head, as sighs of desperation have begun exhaling from your body.

I know, I understand, and I agree, but we're moms, and if we're going to be efficient with our housework, schedules—of all kinds—must be created, implemented and followed as best as possible. Once an organized laundry routine has been established, you'll have mastered one more area of household responsibilities—then that cave of clothes that requires your attention daily may not seem so bad after all. Plus, the helpful habits I'm about to provide you with will preserve the sanity you struggle to keep, all while maintaining a healthy relationship between you and your laundry room. So, try to deal with my annoying scheduling requests just a bit longer . . . and promise you'll at least try them?

Pinky-swear? (Shake your head up and down in a vertical motion.)

Atta girl!

Where were we? Oh, yes. Creating a schedule. Take deep breaths and here we go.

Now, depending on your week and the number of members within your family—not to mention how much time you want to commit to laundry each day—you'll need to develop a program to keep you on track. Remember, piles, heaps, and mounds of laundry are not fun, are very overwhelming, and are likely the cause of additional stress that moms just don't need. Figure out a schedule—you can check out mine below—and proceed accordingly.

Here's how it works in our home, for our family of five:

### *The Sulpizio Schedule of Laundering*

**Monday**: Hubby's duds get washed, dried, cleaned, and put away.
**Tuesday**: Daughter's turn. This girl has a ton of laundry.
**Wednesday**: Son #1 and #2: It's boy's night in the laundry room!
**Thursday**: Mom/towels/sheets: This may take a number of loads!
**Friday–Sunday:** Laundry room is closed (unless any member of the family would like to tackle their laundry . . . on their own that is).

This type of timetable is pretty self-explanatory. Basically, you're dividing your laundry loads on a per-day basis, per each member of your family. It's an easy-to-manage agenda that will have you bidding a final *adieu* to the confusion, and at times, mass hysteria that tends to take place when cleaning clothes. So, head on over to your computer, devise your laundry schedule, and place it in a conspicuous location within your home. Maybe even right there in your laundry room. Oh, and make sure that every member of your family takes notice of the day of the week their laundry will be washed from here on out. No exceptions, no changes, no ifs, ands, or buts, unless of course, those sweet kiddos of yours want to do the laundry themselves.

Yah, that's what I figured.

But wait, there's more.

While we're busy shaking things up in the laundry room, let's provide a few additional rules—though more like guidelines than actual rules—and tips to help us in an effort to cut down on the clothing chaos for good. Not sure what I'm talking about? Let's address the issue of dirty clothes first, and what actually constitutes "soiled" clothing, shall we?

As a female, I'll be the first to admit that I tend to change my clothes a lot during a twenty-four hour period. Whether I'm changing because my current outfit just isn't working for me for whatever reason, or if I actually need to modify my clothing based on an activity I'm about to partake in, I go through a lot of clothes each day . . . too many if we're being honest here.

This unflattering trait appears to be genetic in that my own daughter has seemingly inherited the same issue. From a very early age, my little girl began shedding her outfits in favor of new ones as soon as she could dress herself. It started innocently with princess gowns and dress-up clothing, but quickly moved into casual wear—and this is where the problems began. It's one thing when you change your clean clothes and immediately put them back where they were, it's another when you throw them in the hamper in the hopes that mom will just deal with them, instead. See the problem?

## ENTER THE DIRTY RULE

No matter if you have boys or girls, we all know how laundry tends to pile up. Oftentimes, our children will intentionally throw clean clothes (garments only worn for a short amount of time) into the hamper, instead of hanging them back up in their closets. It seems as though our kids, and maybe even our spouses, need to understand what constitutes "dirty" apparel. And rather than repeating this information time and again, we can provide them with a visual reminder to refer to. Feel free to incorporate these rules into your home—no copyright infringements apply. Scan them in, print them out, and have your family read them, too. Shoot, make it a contract of sorts; but whatever you do, make sure your kids understand the definition of "dirty" as it applies to their clothing. Amen?

Okay, here we go:

- ☆ **Duration**: If you've only worn your outfit for an hour or so—say to church for example—then your clothes are NOT, I repeat, NOT dirty: HANG THEM UP!
- ☆ **Change of plans:** If you tried on an outfit and then decided it just wasn't right for you for that particular moment, hour, or day, your clothes are NOT dirty. HANG THEM UP!
- ☆ **Oops, I did it again:** If you accidentally knocked an article of clothing off of its hanger causing it to fall to the floor of your closet, please don't ignore it with the hopes that Mom will be by shortly to do the job for you. And by all means, do NOT place them in the hamper. These clothes are not dirty. HANG THEM UP!

- ☆ **The gross factor**: If you have worn your clothes all day long (and in some cases only for an hour), have boogers, sweat, tears, blood, food, juice, or any other mystery fluid staining the fabric fibers, please place them in hamper and mom will wash them . . . sometime soon, but there's no guarantee. This type of garment can be considered (*Ding! Ding! Ding!*): DIRTY! PLACE IT IN THE HAMPER.

Now that we've figured out this issue and dealt with it accordingly, it's time to move on and focus our attention on the next one. And it's a doozy! It's a problem that can be considered a crisis of sorts since it causes confusion, mayhem, and threatens to push our patience to the outer limits. I'm referring to none other than the unsolved mystery of (*dun dun dun dun!*) . . . our missing socks.

I'm not sure how it happens, and I have no clue as to why it occurs, but it seems that after every load washed, the same number of socks that went into my washing machine never make it back out of the dryer. Countless pairs of socks have lost their mates in a senseless act that can never be explained—at least not by me. But take note, Wonder Woman Wannabes, because there is, in fact, something that we can do about this.

It's time to take action.

## THE MYSTERY OF THE MISSING SOCKS AND UNRULY UNDIES

> *"I Still Haven't Found What I'm Looking For."*
>
> —U2

You've been there before and understand the frustration I'm speaking of. This type of foul play tends to occur each and every time we wash a load of clothes, now doesn't it? We place a slew of socks into the washing machine, and upon drying and folding, we realize something has gone horribly wrong. It appears that many of our stockings have gone missing; and even though we search high and low for their whereabouts (behind the dryer, under the washer, or possibly hiding in the lint trap), our efforts seem to be in vain. They're gone, without a trace or shred of evidence of any kind—no half-a-sock, cut fibers, unstitched ribbing, nothing! They've vanished and you're left without a clue.

Until now that is.

Here's a little trick that I recently stumbled upon that will provide the much-needed answer to all of your missing sock problems. Now, keep in mind, in order for this strategy to work properly, it must be implemented and executed correctly by each member within your family. Here's what to do.

**Meshes of color:** Grab a mesh bag. Choosing varying colors for each member of the family works best, but if those aren't available, labeled bags will work just as well. Make sure the totes you have purchased are durable and have a zipper or some type of closure that will prevent contents from spilling out.

**To each their own:** Provide one mesh bag per family member, making sure to keep them stored by their hampers or anywhere else they place their laundry.

**Use it or lose it:** Each member of the family is to use their mesh bag as a storage unit for dirty socks, underwear, bras, and swimsuits only.

**Safe and secure:** Come laundry day, these totes can be thrown into the wash, keeping all items secure within, with no chance of losing garments. This also means your days of confusing your boys' socks are long gone. Their underwear? They'll no longer scream when they accidentally put on a pair of 2T skivvies when their body warrants a size six instead. It's an ingenious plan, and your socks will thank you for it—and I bet your little boys will, too.

All right, girls, are you feeling a bit better about your laundering efforts and the amount of time you'll be spending in the laundry room? I sure hope so. But just in case, here are a few more tips you can use.

## MORE BONUS TIPS

Yep. There's more! Consider some of these tidbits when performing laundry duties next:

**Don't wait.** Put away each family member's clothes the same night you wash, dry, and fold them. It's all well and good to place your freshly laundered piles of clothes in laundry baskets until you're motivated to hang them up, but let's be honest girls—this type of system rarely works. Believe me, I know. And, you can even ask your children, the younger ones too, to help with putting their own clothes away. It will save you time and energy once they get the hang of it.

**Check the schedule.** Depending on how you set up your laundry schedule, you may want to tackle your laundry after seven o'clock at night. Most cities have a reduced energy rate that will help you save money if you use the bulk of your appliances after prime-time hours. Check into this at the local level and see how much you can save.

**Keepin' it clean.** Clean your washer and dryer at least once a month. That sounds like an oxymoron of sorts, but refer to your owner's manual to understand how you can best take care of your units. That's definitely worth looking into.

**Dig for gold.** Got change leftover at the end of each wash? Store a piggy bank in your laundry room to save all the loose change you find. Finders, keepers!

**Pick pockets.** Make sure to check the pockets of your kids' clothes prior to putting them in the wash. There's nothing like opening your dryer and noticing your garments have been stained pink by melted lip gloss, or something similar. Save yourself the hassle and make an effort to discover these items prior to "cleaning" them.

**Revamp your laundry room.** Give your laundry room a makeover. We spend a lot of time in that little space, so why not brighten it up with a fresh coat of paint, and a few fun décor items? The simplest things can cheer up any daily task.

**Get your kids involved.** Don't wait until your children are leaving for college to teach them the basics known as Laundry 101. Give them a quick course on how to clean their clothes as soon as they hit double digits—as in ten years of age—or even younger if you think they're ready. By taking over their own laundering needs, this will provide you with some much needed laundry relief, and give them some added responsibility, too. Sign me up!

# 13

# THE AILMENT QUEEN: FIGHTING OFF INFLUENZA, VIRUSES, AND OTHER BOUTS OF NASTINESS

*"God's plans for your life far exceed the circumstances of your day."*

**—Louie Giglio**

Vomit. Diarrhea. Pee. Boogers.

You're probably squirming in your chair at this point, unsure of the *need* to read any further.

But if there's one thing we moms are particularly knowledgeable about, it's dealing with nasty ailments and the four bodily fluids that every mommy dreads in her tenure as a parent. I mean, no matter how hard we try, how much we pray, or how fast we can run, sooner or later there's no escaping the fact that we'll inevitably fall victim to these Mystery Fluids of Horror. You've undoubtedly already experienced numerous "run-in's" of your own . . . puke-laden blouses, peed-on pants, pooped-on shoes, and boogers in places where boogers should never be. Hey, sometimes being the mommy can be downright gross indeed, but dealing with ailing kiddos is just part of our job description—whether we can stomach it or not.

Having said all that, I'll come clean and admit that if there's one thing that makes me want to don a cape and inherit some sort of superhuman power, it's taking care of my poor babies when they're sick. I mean, I have issues when they spike a fever, I struggle when a coughing fit attacks, and I flat-out despise when influenza (or something similar) invades one of their little bodies . . . or two . . . or three . . . or even me!

But if there's one pet peeve that threatens my sanity above all others, it would have to be anything—and I mean everything—dealing with the regurgitation of food. Without a doubt, hands-down, barf is this mama's kryptonite. And although I've been subject to my mortal enemy too many times to count, the mere sight of this menace still causes me to fall weak in the knees, and I become anxiously aware that I might be days, if not hours away from the same type of fate. Fortunately, I've fared much better in my bouts with the barfs than I ever would have thought possible—praise God. I've even managed to keep my food down, my stomach settled, and my heart and mind fully devoted to my poor kiddo(s) while tending to their physical needs. That's just what moms do. It's our calling, how we were created to be. But like you, I've also stood by as nasty ailments ruined trips, wrecked holidays, and provided us with memories we'd rather forget than take the time to remember.

Who else can relate?

## NOT-SO-MEMORABLE MOMENTS

As mommies, there are numerous life events that we just can't wait to experience through the eyes of our children. It may be their first Christmas, or their first trip to the zoo, or for some of us (author raises hand), it might be their very first pair of Superhero Underoos. No matter what it is though, it's safe to say that we look forward to participating in as many of our children's "firsts" as we possibly can. But what happens when these memories become threatened by a stomach ailment, the flu, a nasty cold, or some other mucous-inducing sickness? Needless to say, illnesses can wreak havoc on family time as our poor kiddos—and quite possibly the rest of our family—get infected, invaded, and devastated.

Case in point: when my two eldest children were toddlers, I decided I could wait no longer and had (*had!*) to take them on their first outing to "The Happiest Place on Earth." I spent a lot of time planning this trip, mapping out the sights I wanted them to see, and circling the various areas within the park I wanted to take them to. Let's just say that I had anticipated this vacation for a very long time and could hardly wait for my own kids to see the site where some of my favorite childhood memories took place. As we embarked upon our journey, the first day couldn't have gone any better. My children were behaving well, the crowds were minimal, and the weather was sublime. Everything was going along so splendidly that my husband and I found ourselves anticipating what the second day of our adventure had in store for us.

But that's when things went horribly wrong.

After a long day of sight-seeing and fun, we decided to invest in some souvenirs and made our way into a gift shop located just outside of the park. As it turned out, this wasn't such a good idea. After denying my daughter's request for a new tiara, tantrum mode set in. Feet were flying, arms were flailing, and her screaming—which sounded more like shrieking—sent all the neighborhood canines in the city of Anaheim howling. This girl was in full meltdown mode and it was extremely apparent that I needed to leave the store ASAP. I immediately retreated outside so my husband could relieve me of her massive fit and I could tend to our toddler son instead. But in the instant that I picked my little guy up—after dealing with my temporarily possessed daughter—*it* happened. Without any sort of warning, my sweet boy opened his mouth and launched his $10.99 nachos all over me. I was stunned, soaked, gasping for some fresh air, and praying that his unexpected regurgitation wouldn't initiate the onset of my own. My poor Disney tee took the brunt of his now-vacant belly, and the world's favorite little fairy that graced the front of my shirt had just been doused with something other than pixie dust.

The lesson in all of this—and my point in telling you such a story—is that our children are going to become ill from time to time. They're going to have bouts with viruses, issues with diarrhea, and colds that produce an endless supply of snot. We can't predict these events, nor are we privy to the information as to when . . . or where . . . they may strike. But if I know anything, it's this: having a child under the weather is extremely hard on us moms. It can find us crippled with worry, and send us straight to our knees in prayer. It can disrupt our normally scheduled programming, have us frantically calling the pediatrician at weird hours of the day, and may even land us a spot in the emergency room during the middle of the night. I for one can't help the fact that each time an illness takes over one of my kiddo's bodies, my thinking immediately resorts to the worst. My Christian faith tells me otherwise and begs me to place my trust in God, but my mind still races, panic sets in, and it's all I can do to remain calm in an effort to figure out what to do next.

It's at times like these I can't help but ask: Why couldn't God have called me to become a doctor? A nurse? Or somebody with a skill set including some sort of medical knowledge at least?

It appears He had other plans in mind.

## IS THERE A DOCTOR IN THE HOUSE?

Why does he have a fever? Why is she coughing so much? Why do his eyes look different? Why is her lip puffy? How did that pencil become lodged up his nose? These are all questions I've asked myself on occasion, after enduring such instances with my own children. My impatient mind demands an immediate response, while my anxious nerves desperately need the calming peace that can only come from knowing my child will be all right. As I've mentioned before, there's no doctor residing in my house, nor is there one living next door, around the corner, or within a two-mile radius of my home.

So what do most of us do when we're in need of a medical solution?

Well, other than seeking prayer, many of us mistakenly run to the Internet—and the medical Web sites contained there—in order to get the answers we so urgently crave.

Take it from me—this may not be the best idea.

Sometimes, using the Internet to help preliminarily "diagnose" what may or may not be ailing our children can be a helpful tool—as far as the wealth of information that's provided there. For me, though, and more often than not, the World Wide Web becomes a means for added concern and worry. Oftentimes, symptoms reported can be said to be as minor as a cold . . . or something as major as cancer, of all things. Needless to say, the Internet is the one place where we can find information—whether right, wrong, or slightly misguided—but one that can also cause our minds to race with improper diagnoses and major anxiety.

So what *should* we do?

Even though we may not be physicians or medical gurus of any kind, we are, in fact, the first responders within our home. We are in charge of deciding how urgent medical attention should occur and how soon a call into the pediatrician is warranted. But in order to do so effectively, we need information first. We need to devise our own set of questions with which to equip ourselves and our children's medical providers, in order to provide the necessary information they'll need to further assist us, and our little ones. By creating this mental checklist, you can better assess the situation and decide on the best course of action to take . . . all without entering a crazed state of paranoia.

The best thing to do when our children are sick is to take a few deep breaths, evaluate the situation we're dealing with, pray, and then take the appropriate actions.

Peruse this mental checklist, commit it to memory, and apply it the next time a bout with "bugs" rears its ugly head.

The Mental Medical Checklist—for Moms:

- ☆ Are they bleeding? If so, where?
- ☆ Do they have a fever? If so, how high?
- ☆ Are they barfing? (*Please, no!*) How often?
- ☆ Are they peeing and pooping normally? If not, note it.
- ☆ Are they lethargic?
- ☆ Are they sleeping too little? Too much?
- ☆ Are they eating and drinking regularly?
- ☆ How is their behavior/attitude?
- ☆ How are their eyes? Pupils dilating normally? Any "gunk" to note?
- ☆ Does breathing appear to be regular?
- ☆ Any bruising or swelling? Where?
- ☆ Are there any bones protruding out of their skin? (If not, this is usually a very good sign.)
- ☆ Is there anything they can't move or apply pressure to?

The answers to these questions can be extremely helpful in determining the necessary means of action when our kids are ailing. Remember: always remain calm, follow your gut instinct, and when in doubt, always seek medical advice, attention, and assistance.

Oh, and one more thing. Seek solace in the fact that in times like these, God is always just a chat away. Set your sights on Him, and give your worries to Him. Keep in mind that He'll give you the strength and wisdom to deal with whatever illness your kiddos (or you) are facing . . . yes, even *if* puke is involved.

## WHEN MAMA IS NAUSEATED: BATTLING *BIG* BUGS

Taking care of your children when *they're* sick is hard enough as it is, but trying to take care of your kids when *you're* sick is an entirely different story, isn't it? When mama can't get out of bed, everyone and everything tends to suffer. All efforts to maintain the regularly scheduled programming of meal planning, cleaning, and a strict laundry routine are completely cast aside, and it's as if our homes are literally turned upside down. The housework piles up, the kids are running amuck, and all we can do is lay there in the fetal position, lethargic, zapped of all of our energy . . . and completely useless.

At this point, there's no denying that we're in need of some serious assistance. No matter if it's a relative, spouse, or family friend—when mommy's ailing, we girls are in need of a reliable caretaker to see that our children are fed, clothed, and (somewhat) clean. We need help getting our kids to school, activities, appointments, engagements, and so on. But for Wonder Woman Wannabes, who struggle to ask for help in the first place, this can seem like an impossible task to accomplish. We feel awkward, uncomfortable, and more often than not, we'd just rather deal with it ourselves rather than having to bother anyone else. Is any of this sounding familiar?

Listen up, ladies, because it's in these moments that we need to ditch our Supermom tendencies and call in some reinforcements. Not even Wonder Woman herself could claim victory over vomiting without enlisting some help from her Super Friends. So let's forget about our need for perfection, rid ourselves of any pride we're holding onto, and devise an emergency back-up plan for when Supermom—I'm talking about you here—is super sick.

## TIME FOR SOME BACK-UP— A PACT FOR HELPING A SICK SISTER OUT:

*"I get by with a little help from my friends."*

**—The Beatles**

My mom lives over two thousand miles away, and my husband? Well, he has a job that requires a lot of traveling throughout the year. My immediate support system is, how should I put it? Totally nil. That means, if this Wonder Woman Wannabe is going down—as in becoming prey to a nasty virus or other illness—I have to rely on the assistance of my local gal pals to temporarily relieve me from my mommy responsibilities in order to achieve some mama-get-well time. Yep, this is where you and your best girls need to band together, devise a plan, and get prepared to help a sick sister out when the need arises.

It's time for the Buddy Back-Up Plan.

Now, the idea here is pretty simple: you're basically setting up a structured schedule detailing your children's activities and events, should your health suddenly decide to go South for a day or so. By discussing this with your friend(s) and devising a system that works for all involved, you are teaming up to make sure that, should the need arise, your kiddos are covered. But in order to be effective, these plans have to be detailed and well thought-out. They must be updated frequently and consistently, because you never know when you're going to get ill; and if your plan isn't ready when you need it, chaos—like we discussed before—will most definitely ensue. Which is the last thing we want to endure when we're sick.

Now remember, when making your master plan, there are a number of things to take into consideration, as well as some questions to answer when doing so. For instance, you'll want to make sure you're providing your friends with enough information in order to execute this plan without a thousand phone calls to you during the day. To get such a program up and running, follow these simple by-laws:

**Select your friends.** Talk to your friends and see which and how many of them are willing to participate. Make a pact with one another, because all parties involved need to be able and willing to follow through on this agreement.

**Set guidelines/rules.** All members within your group need to decide upon and agree to the terms you've outlined and established. Note: this sounds much more "legal" than it really is.

**Make a plan.** Each member within your group will be required to set up their own, personalized schedule, calendar, or other detailed list of information for each child who will need tending to while mom is ill (see my example below). This can, and should, include all necessary contact information, details about afterschool activities, and/or special instructions your kids will require.

**Be thorough.** Anything and everything you deem to be important information needs to be listed on your plan. Do your kids have allergies? If so, what kind, how badly, and what type of special medications are required? As far as afterschool activities go, what type of equipment do your children need? When and where are their practices and games? Make sure to include a calendar? Again, the more information provided, the better your friends will be able to help you.

**Be prepared.** Aside from calendars, schedules, and detailed lists, your Buddy Back-Up Plan should also include a set amount of cash to cover dinner out for the kids and gas money for your friend.

## THE BUDDY BACK-UP PLAN

*Contact Information:*

| Contact | Home/Main Phone | Cell Phone | Address | Email |
|---|---|---|---|---|
| Dad | 555-1212 | 555-1213 | 1820 Superhero Ln. | mls@mls.com |
| Mom | | | | |
| Pediatrician | | | | |
| Other | | | | |

Other contacts/information:

*School Information:*

| Child's Name | School | School Address | School Phone Number | Teacher's Name | Teacher's Email |
|---|---|---|---|---|---|
| Sara | Ryan Elem | 1212 State Dr. | 555-1212 | Ms. Bliss | ms.bliss@ msbliss.com |
| | | | | | |
| | | | | | |
| | | | | | |
| | | | | | |

Special Drop-Off/Pick-Up Instructions:

*Afterschool Activities:*

| Child | Activity | Time | Day | Place | Address | Instructor | Attire |
|---|---|---|---|---|---|---|---|
| Sara | Ballet | 5:00 | M, W | The Studio | 4454 Tutu Lane | Ms. Mary | Tutu/ Leotard |
| | | | | | | | |
| | | | | | | | |
| | | | | | | | |

Special Instructions:

*Other Info:*

| Child | Allergies | Medications | Food Issues | Other |
|---|---|---|---|---|
| Sara | Bees | n/a | Dislikes Honey | |
| | | | | |
| | | | | |
| | | | | |

Special Instructions:

Remember, it's up to you and your friends to decide how in depth your plan should go, and how you'll arrange to serve each other in your times of need. By setting up a system such as this, and by being prepared when sickness strikes, not only will you be less stressed, but you'll also be able to focus on getting better, quicker. And isn't that the point in the first place? As moms, we've got to take care of ourselves, ask for help when we need it, and be there for our "sisters in the trenches" when we're called upon.

> *"Carry each other's burdens, and in this way you will fulfill the law of Christ."*
>
> **—Galatians 6:2**

## EXTRA TIPS:

Got bugs? Here are a few extra tips to help you and your family deal when those nasty illnesses invade:

**Vitamins:** Make sure you and your kiddos are taking plenty of vitamins, especially during the winter months. As mentioned before, I am not a doctor, nor am I anywhere even close; but I do recommend seeking physician approval prior to initiating a vitamin regimen of your own. Seek assistance and find out which supplements are best for you, your kids, and your spouse. Get and stay healthy!

**Soap:** Use soap, and lots of it. Make sure your children are constantly washing their hands and attempting some type of hygiene routine in order to keep those nasty, sickness-invoking germs far, far away.

**Doctor:** Have your doctor on speed dial on your landline, as well as in your cell phone contacts. The doctor should be listed *ahead* of your favorite pizza parlor. Just sayin'.

**The "pukies":** When your kids have a case of "the pukies," make sure to designate an official "barf bowl" to keep by their beds in case of an emergency. Oh, and use a waterproof mattress cover as well. Spills happen. *Ew!*

**Sick day:** Purchase a special "sickie" mask or dress in costume in order to uplift your children's spirits when they aren't feeling like their normal selves. Not only will it brighten their moods, but what kid *wouldn't* like their chicken soup served from their favorite cape-clad superhero? Side note: incorporating a mask into said costume might also help keep their yucky "bugs" from invading your healthy body. Word to the wise!

**The plan:** Work on the Buddy Back-Up Plan right now. Store it in your family binder or with any other important documents you have so that it's ready and waiting for use in your time of need. Update as needed.

14

# COUPON CLIPPING, SUPERHERO STYLE: SAVING MOOLA & MAINTAINING A BUDGET

*"I've got a coupon for that!"*

**—Unknown**

Whether it be shopping for groceries, clothing, home décor, or any other item that we're in the market for, there's nothing quite like discovering one's inner discount diva by enjoying some amazing deals and superb steals. Not to mention the recognition that comes along with being dubbed the honorary queen of the retail scene—a title most worthy of some sort of praise, don't you think? Right or wrong, I do have to confess that, for me, discounted retail therapy provides somewhat of a "natural high," if you will. I mean, to be able to walk into a store, coupons in tow, and leave with a full bag of market merchandise and lots of cash still left in the old wallet, is nothing short of awesome. It can feel as though I've conquered the retail world (as I flex my biceps and take a bow) . . . all by redeeming a few vouchers and saving some sweet cents.

Apparently, I'm not alone in my feelings either, because the art, hobby, and the obsession revolving around the couponing craze has taken our nation by storm in recent years. Millions of women and men alike have set out for the sole purpose of getting their pantries stocked, all while keeping their wallets full. Yep. Couponing is everywhere, and if you have yet to jump on the frugal bandwagon—but are perhaps toying with the idea of getting started—allow me to provide you with the ins and outs you'll need to know in order to initiate your new pastime, and save your family some major dollars in the process.

But be forewarned.

You see, this crazed state of couponing is not as easy as it looks. It happens to require a decent amount of time, not to mention discipline and superb organizational skills. And should I dare mention the use of mathematics as well? *Yikes!* In fact, Hot Coupon World posted an article in March 2011—"Extreme Couponing versus Hardcore Couponing"; Google it—reporting that their members spend an average of fourteen hours a week devoted to this art of saving money.

Fourteen hours per week? Considering that we moms have a total of 168 hours during this time frame to take care of our families, homes, and maybe even ourselves, it appears that we need to gauge just how important saving money at the store really is. If you're thinking that coupon clipping isn't worth your time, that it's too much of a distraction in general, then by all means don't second-guess it; just move on. But if you're contemplating the idea of becoming a voucher-clad money-saving machine, then continue reading.

But don't say I didn't warn you.

## SCENES AT THE SUPERMARKET

It was a dark and stormy night. Or maybe it was a sunny, summer day. I can't remember—dark and stormy with a touch of thunder and a hint of rain sounds good to me. Let's continue.

*"She watches over the affairs of her household and does not eat from the bread of idleness."*

**—Proverbs 31:27**

I was stuck at the grocery store picking up five items (no more, no less) that were necessary for the latest dinner concoction I was brewing at home. My youngest son was also afoot, and impulsively ransacking the breath-freshening section at the checkout stand as I approached the self-checkout kiosk to buy my groceries.

I quickly scanned my purchases, got my debit card out and waited for the nice, computer-generated voice to ask me a series of questions in order to complete my shopping experience.

"Do you have any coupons?" she asked me quizzically.

*Coupons?* I scoffed, rolling my eyes at the mere mention of such a suggestion. *Who has time for coupons?* I thought. I certainly didn't, nor did I want to spend any of my personal time perusing advertisements, Web sites, and flyers in search of a twenty-cent coupon, of all things. Add the pressure of having to physically remember these vouchers—and actually use them prior to their expiration date. I had made the decision long ago that couponing was one aspect of bargain shopping I wanted nothing to do with. Besides, I had better things to do with my time, didn't I?

I pushed the "proceed to checkout" option on the computer screen without hesitation. I just needed to get my groceries and get home.

But after snatching my receipt, my merchandise, and my now minty-fresh, gum-toting son, something grabbed my attention that I just couldn't ignore. Out of the corner of my eye—dang that peripheral vision—I saw what appeared to be one of those extreme couponing people. Up front and in the flesh, there she was, in all of her voucher-redeeming glory. Now, I had heard of men and women like this who could literally purchase their groceries for free, all because they spent hour upon hour searching for deals and clipping coupons. However, prior to this occurrence, I had never actually seen such a display, and honestly considered the idea of an "extreme couponer" to be an urban legend of sorts . . . a myth. Not like a unicorn or Sasquatch per se, but something I definitely thought I would never encounter in person. But there she stood, with her grocery carts—six of them in all, filled to maximum capacity—and her entourage waiting on stand-by for the final tally.

I immediately ditched my urgency to return home as I made my way through the crowd, and attempted to get closer look at what this discount diva was all about. What I saw was mind-blowing. Not only did she have coupons, eighty-thousand of them or so, but this woman was carrying the most elaborate organizational system I had ever seen. Coupon after coupon held together in a huge binder, broken down and sorted by date, expiration, and brand. It. Was. A. Masterpiece. I mean, this lady had it together and appeared to be a celebrity of sorts, as all eyes in line behind her waited for the store clerk to read her final tender.

"That will be $4.18," the cashier uttered, her eyes glazed over and hands clenched shut from processing so many coupons through the scanner.

The crowd began to cheer as the couponing queen began giving out high-fives to her new and completely devoted grocery store fan base. —Okay, so maybe that's a slight exaggeration, but there was no denying that this gal was reveling in her sweet savings and all of the hard work she had invested prior to this shopping extravaganza.

It was at that point that I peered down at my one, measly shopping bag that contained my $18.58 purchase. I had no-onlookers, no devoted fans (except my doting son), and no one to high-five for my lack of thriftiness that day. I just had a single bag of really expensive groceries that I paid way too much for. It was evident from that moment forward that I needed to hop on this couponing bandwagon and attempt to save my family some money. Yes, it was time to flex my discount-saving muscles and tackle this couponing craze once and for all.

But how was an amateur like me going to get started? Well, it was finally time to figure it out.

## TO COUPON OR NOT TO COUPON: THAT IS THE QUESTION

In an effort to start saving, I retreated to the World Wide Web after returning home from the store that day. What I found was total coupon chaos as I became extremely overwhelmed by the wealth of information in front of me. I was confused, intimidated, slightly frustrated. And it appeared that taking these first small steps toward becoming a discount diva was not only going to be tough, but might just cause my sanity to waiver a bit in the process. You know—the kind of crazy where you want to yank your hair out and scream at the top of your lungs?

Where were the shortcuts? Why didn't they have buy one, get one free coupons on the items I used? And what in the heck was a stockpile? Was I involuntarily entering the realm of new age hoarding or something? These questions and more flooded my brain as I became consumed with frustration. I mean, all I was looking for was the opportunity to grab a few deals. I didn't necessarily want to spend a huge portion of my life clipping out coupons, organizing them, or planning out my shopping trips. But it was fairly evident from the get-go that the couponing kingdom was going to require some fairly intense labor if I was going to be successful at it.

But as I managed to find out from my initial attempts as a voucher-redeeming mommy, "successful" certainly wouldn't be the correct word to describe my initiation into my extreme-savings adventure.

It turned out that I was bad at couponing.

Is that even possible?

Apparently, in my case, it is.

## NOT SO "SUPER" AT THE SUPERMARKET

*"Plans fail for lack of counsel,*
*but with many advisers they succeed."*

**—Proverbs 15:22**

My first attempts at my latest pastime were anything but heroic. In fact, as upsetting as it is to admit, my primary stab at saving some cash ended in complete failure . . . we're talking below-average merits here. Yep. It appeared that my dreams of earning free groceries, and maybe a short stint as a celebrity extreme-couponing queen, had instead turned into a money-saving nightmare.

Wanna know why?

I was doing it all wrong.

I ended up spending *more* money on my groceries *with* coupons than I would have without them. Did you read what I just wrote? My crack at couponing actually ended up costing me cash instead of saving me some. There wasn't a stockpile to speak of, nor any savings to boast about. In fact, rather than recouping a massive amount of monies on items I could use, I came home with five tubes of toothpaste in a flavor that immediately engages the gag reflex; ten candy bars (because I *needed* those?); and a huge pack of ultra-absorbent, adult incontinence pads that I hope and pray I will never have to use but still managed to buy anyway, all because I had a coupon.

It was apparent that I had no clue what I was doing and couldn't help but think that maybe this couponing craze wasn't intended for *this* mom. Maybe I just couldn't get a handle on all of the associated tips, hints, and rules. Maybe my organizational skills weren't up to par. And maybe purchasing five thousand items for a mere twenty-four cents just wasn't meant to be . . . for me.

Or maybe, just maybe here, I wasn't given the right tools in order to successfully realize a discounted shopping trip in the first place. Perhaps I needed to perform some further research—sit down and really pay attention to the rules governing the coupon nation in order to redeem monetary benefits from it.

Yah, maybe that was it. I just needed to know how to get started and then soak up all the advice I could in order to reap such merits, no matter how intimidating it might be. I mean, there's a lot to learn and varying strategies on partaking productively in the voucher-redeeming game. So, if you've yet to delve into this fascinating world or if you've been burned in the checkout line before by going about the coupon craze all wrong, let me give you the dos and don'ts, and a few tips, on this money-saving hobby.

## RULE #1: SALES ARE CYCLICAL

Cyclical? As in a circle? Yep, think of merchandise markdowns as traveling in a 360 degree fashion, around and around, over and over again. There is indeed a pattern to promotional sales—something that every discount diva in training must take note of and plan accordingly for. For instance, say you just purchased a gallon of milk on sale this week at your local grocery store. Chances are this exact product will be reduced once again, just three to four weeks later. See? Cyclical. This means that the coupons you've been clipping should be used in conjunction with the sales offered by your grocer to ensure that you glean additional savings. The more money you can save the better. So, get up to date on current promotions, markdowns, and clearances for the market you're shopping at, as well as the pattern of sales they're sporting.

## RULE #2: TIME TO GET ORGANIZED

Every couponing queen will admit that the key to becoming successful at this craft is by understanding the importance of true organization. Generally speaking, couponing is all about keeping track of your savings, your spending, and the structured stash of coupons you possess. Whether you opt to use a binder, basket, tote, crate, or a mixture of all these items, you'll want to invest enough time into implementing a system that will work best for you—one where you'll be able to locate your coupons quickly and in an organized fashion.

But where you keep your coupons is just the beginning. How you organize these clippings is another story. Invest in dividers with tabs, and select how you'll want to store your vouchers—whether it be by brand, expiration date, store aisle, type of item, or by the market in which they can be used. There is no wrong way to do this, but you must consider which option will best keep you on track—as opposed to making you totally frazzled. Remember: organization is key to proclaiming victory in your money-saving efforts.

## RULE #3: DO YOUR RESEARCH

As a coupon-toting mama, organizing your stash is only half the battle. The other half? Well, that would be understanding how it all works. The ins and outs of voucher-redeeming, if you will. I'll be honest—it kind of makes my head spin. Not all the way around mind you, but enough to get me confused, and slightly lightheaded. Make sure you understand a little bit (okay, who am I kidding . . . a lot) of the following information prior to starting this game.

**Rules and regulations:** Yep, each and every store has a set of rules, a policy, when it comes to redeeming your coupons, and not all markets are the same. So, you know what that means? You need to have a copy of those grocer's rules and by-laws with you to ward off issues at checkout. Print off a copy—they're located on the store's Web site or you can ask for them at the customer service desk—and keep them in your handy-dandy coupon notebook for easy and quick reference. Read often and check for updated policies as needed.

**Map it out:** It's time to consider your shopping trips a treasure hunt for adults, because couponing can be made simpler by understanding the layout of the store in which you shop. I'll admit: I don't do very well with maps—or directions, or any other sort of navigational tools—but you may find that a store blueprint can be of great assistance in making your shopping trips smoother and quicker. Print one off, or seek out the customer service desk, and keep it with you and reference as often as possible. Again, devise a system that will work best for you.

**Double the fun:** Some stores still offer double coupons—which means, double the money off. *Hello!* Many merchants have gotten away from this practice or only offer such discounts on certain days of the week. Find out when these days are and schedule your shopping trips around them. It pays to be in the know, girls, so freshen up on your store's policies and learn what their rules are regarding the elusive and oh-so-tantalizing double coupons.

**Flyers in tow:** Each and every week, participating grocery stores and pharmacies advertise their discounted items for the rest of the week, both in stores and online. Now, this is where you're going to need to sharpen your detective-like skills prior to your shopping endeavors. You see, in order to really capitalize on these markdowns, you'll need to investigate these sales well before you step foot into the store.

At this point, you may be wondering why.

Well, say you have a coupon for fifty cents off when you buy two cans of tomato soup. After checking your local merchant's flyer, they are having a sale on the same exact soup you've got a coupon for. *Cha-ching*! See, by doing your homework and combining store sales with your clipped vouchers, you'll be able to really make a dent in your grocery bill and save, save, save. So, make sure you do your research, visit your grocer's Web sites for their weekly sales, match your coupons to current price reductions, and then get to shopping and a whole bunch of saving. *Woo hoo!*

**Make me a match:** As mentioned, always do your research before heading out to shop, keeping those store flyers in tow. The reason is simple: price matching! Oftentimes, in an effort to compete with other markets, retailers will match the sale price of an identical item at another store by giving it to you at the competitor's price. For instance, if the Fish Warehouse is having their bi-annual blowout sale on tuna fish for a mere twenty cents a can, but you're currently halfway across town shopping at Murphy's Market where they're a whopping forty cents more per can, chances are Murphy's will honor the competitor's pricing—and honor a coupon on top of the sales price if you have one. But be prepared. The oh-so-savvy shopper in you may have to cough up proof of Fish Warehouse's sale price. So, have those ads handy and refer to them often while shopping. Have questions about matching? Check your store's policy or chat with the shop's manager—you know, somewhere in all that free time you have, of course.

**Get a "sub":** Meaning—purchase a discounted "sub"scription to your local newspaper. Every Sunday, coupons circulate with the newspaper and most, if not all, paper subscriptions have special deals just for couponing gals like you and me. Call your local paper and see what subscription specials they have to offer and what will fit into your budget.

## RULE #4: COUPONERS KNOW HOW TO PARTY

Okay, you might laugh at the sound of this, but the ladies on the couponing scene are no strangers to a good voucher-trading social from time to time. And there's good reason for this. If you think about it, there are at least a million or so men and women currently vested in saving their families money—and never paying full retail again if they can help it. You can understand this mission, and most certainly can relate to it too . . . so why not throw a shin-dig to help celebrate these efforts. (Like one needs an excuse to get social and eat cake, right?) By attending such gatherings, not only will you meet other money-saving divas—and dudes—but you'll also be able to exchange coupons that you may not have a use for, but another attendee just might. This is known as "trading," and soirées such as these allow couponers to meet, share tips and tricks, and exchange coupons as needed. It's trading at its best!

## RULE #5: THERE'S AN APP FOR THAT

These days, with the likes of modern technology, it appears that there's quite possibly an app for anything and everything. And when it comes to the world of couponing, there are certainly no exceptions. Now, I would be lying if I told you that smartphones weren't extraordinarily helpful when it comes to assisting with saving you money. Need help budgeting? There's an app for that. Need a list of store flyers because you forgot yours at home? Yep, there's an app for that, too. By enlisting your smartphone and investing in a few apps, saving money will never again be so easy . . . or convenient for that matter. Gotta love it!

## RULE #6: DID SOMEONE SAY FREE SAMPLE?

I love—as in *L-O-V-E!*—me a free sample. And I see nothing wrong with heading to those huge discount stores each and every Saturday morning in order to score myself some free food and test out the latest and greatest in new products to hit the market. As it turns out, most of these sampling stations also provide their patrons with coupons toward future purchases of the item being introduced. But keep in mind that free samples aren't *just* limited to in-store visits. It also appears that pro-bono trials are plastered all over the Internet—for those willing to search for and sign-up for them. Interested in learning more? Check out the Web, make sure the security you're running on your computer is up to date, and sign up for some free samples. Couldn't hurt, could it, and who doesn't like something for free? Certainly not me.

## RULE #7: THAT'S SO BUDGET

Sticking to a budget can be a lot harder than it looks, believe me. But there are many tricks to this trade that can help us consumers stay on track with our finances and resist the urge to overspend. A monthly budget—you know, a set amount of money we intend to spend on specific items during any given month—can be a lot easier to adhere to than, for instance, not having one at all. And once you begin the budgeting process, you'll be amazed, not only by the amount of money you're saving each month, but also by the number of dollars wasted in the store by not having implemented this tool sooner.

So, in order to maintain a budget, we must first learn what establishing one looks like. If you have yet to conduct a monthly financial plan yourself, Dave Ramsey (www.daveramsey.com) offers series and studies outlining this very thing. His Web site and step-by-step proposal also provide free, downloadable forms you can use in order to balance your finances and prevent extra spending on a monthly basis. Check it out and follow some of his simple rules.

**Step by step:** Planning a grocery budget isn't necessarily all that easy, but it is a task that proves to be helpful, as well as necessary for saving money. The first step is to take an average of what you spend each month and try and reduce it—slowly. For instance, if you spend $400 per month at the grocery store, try lowering your bill by just ten dollars each trip, keeping your bi-weekly trips to just $190 (for a total monthly bill of $380). Attempt to cut another ten dollars from subsequent trips the following month, and slowly but surely you'll be able to make a significant dent in your grocery bill. Enforcing a realistic budget that you can stick to is extremely important.

**Carry cash:** This one is a bit hard for me to do because I almost never carry a supply of cash in my wallet. There's a reason for this. It seems as though anytime I have a twenty dollar bill in tow, it tends to get spent quickly and on things I just don't need. But, if we're not careful, this is also true when it comes to using credit cards, checks, and debit cards when out shopping. It's much easier to swipe a card at checkout and not worry too much if you go over budget, as opposed to carrying a set amount of cash and only spending what you have allotted for. Allbeit tough, this can be achieved by investing in a cheap calculator and adding up the items you place in your cart as you go.

Warning: if you are going to tackle this tip, I recommend visiting the store by yourself, without the kiddos in tow, and taking the designated amount of cash out of the bank immediately prior to your trip. This will help maintain your concentration, keep you focused, reduce spending, and most importantly, preserve your sanity. Love that.

**Trim the excess:** By establishing and maintaining a budget, it will be easy to see where your family can trim some of the excess spending you may be entertaining each month. By understanding where your money is going, you're more likely to spend less and exercise frugality in the process. Not to say that you're not already the queen of thrift, but as I've already mentioned, setting up a budget can help us gals understand the importance of how and where we spend our moola. Just by checking out your bank statements, you can tell if you've hit the drive-thru too many times this pay period or whether those trips to the craft store are becoming too frequent and maybe a bit too pricey, as well.

**Buy only what you need:** I've said it before, but as tempting as it might be to purchase non-essential items, try and resist the urge—especially when it comes to couponing. If you don't need four jars of extra hot jalapenos, then ditch the voucher and buy one jar instead. Trade the coupon at your next coupon soirée and be on your way. Cut out the excess and you'll, in turn, save a decent amount of money.

*Whew!* Doesn't all of this seem like a lot to know? I mean, at first it seems overwhelming, doesn't it? But as with anything in our lives, once you've done your research and established a system—both organizational and habitual—you'll be saving money with ease in no time at all. Plus, if you get stuck or need some extra help on your super-saving journey, the Internet is just a click away. There you'll find hundreds of Web sites, blogs, webinars, and other types of helpful aids and tutorials that can assist you in succeeding with discounted shopping.

So go ahead and give couponing a try. Seek out friends, church members, or anyone else who has mastered this hobby, and benefit from the knowledge and experience they possess as well . . . because isn't it about time that we start getting some sweet deals at the supermarket? Lord knows we spend enough time and money there already. Amen!

# SECTION III

# THE WONDER WOMAN WANNABE RECLAIMS HER IDENTITY (WELL . . . SORT OF)

# 15

# LET'S GET PHYSICAL: THE WANNABE HITS THE GYM

*"Going to the gym is great for your body, but it's also great for your mind."*

**—Rory McIlroy**

Treadmills, elliptical machines, free weights, and aerobics classes . . . *ahhh*, I must be referring to the gym! The one place this Wonder Woman Wannabe has avoided since she first became a mom.

It wasn't intentional, though . . . at least that's what I kept telling myself for so many years.

But the moment I became pregnant with my daughter was also the instant where "dates" with my exercise facility came to a screeching halt. As an expectant mom, I was worried about exercising too hard, possibly hurting my baby, causing too much stress on my body, and a slew of other excuses I came up with in order to validate my fears and pacify those wacky hormones of mine. Besides, back then, I knew that once I delivered my child, workouts would indeed resume, just as I knew the motivation to get my post-baby body back into shape would return. Not only that, but I also had some pretty high expectations for the type of workout diva I would undoubtedly become. I envisioned myself capable of running a marathon, enduring triathlons, and participating in competitions that would require this body of mine to be physically fit. My children would become my cheering section, holding up signs on the sidelines and rooting me on to the finish line.

But it didn't exactly transpire this way.

Instead, I became sedentary, and slightly comatose, as I opted to spend any free time I had cozied up on my couch, plugged into the latest reality TV show, consuming food, and continually making excuses for why working out just wasn't necessary. I never stepped foot back into the gym and unfortunately for me, the only "exercise" I got consisted of hurried jaunts back and forth between the 'fridge and my sofa. I had no drive, no motivation, and any muscle tone that I had once possessed, was completely gone.

But not even muscle atrophy provided enough incentive to get me off that couch.

Instead, I concocted reasons in order to justify my laziness: I didn't have the time, it cost too much money, the location of the nearest gym was too far away. I even went so far as telling myself that sweating would be too much of an inconvenience, and that lifting weights might cause me to become a bit too "manly" and way too muscular. Yep. All of these reasons (and more) kept me sidelined, couch-ridden, and still eating. And no matter how many times I told myself that each day would be the beginning to a brand new me, you know—the day where I decidedly put down the food and picked up a dumbbell—well, it never happened. Each day got postponed to the next, and pretty soon those days had turned into weeks, weeks transformed into months, and the months quickly turned into years. And I never got off my butt. Not with baby number two or even number three.

> *"If it's important to you, you'll find a way, not an excuse."*
>
> **—Peter Shankman**

You see, like a lot of moms, I got so busy worrying about everyone else and every other thing that I made little-to-no time for little old me and my needs. I allowed myself to make lame excuses and fell into the trap that a lot of moms find themselves in. Rather than scramble to try and find my way out, I let it consume me.

Silly girl, exercise is a must for moms.

Unfortunately for me, so were the excuses . . .

## NO MORE EXCUSES

> *"Beauty is not in the face,*
> *beauty is a light in the heart."*
>
> **—Kahlil Gibran**

As a media-obsessed culture, we've all grown fairly accustomed to the numerous infomercials that plague our regularly scheduled programming ad nauseum. Oftentimes, and usually right around the first of the year, these programs flood the airways as we're subjected to the latest and greatest in exercise products and fads. And for whatever reason, these advertisements just so happen to air when one of us—*okay, me!*—*might* be consuming some type of unhealthy product while seated on the couch, feet propped up, and relaxing from a hectic day spent in the motherhood.

But I can remember one day in particular when, rather than grabbing for my remote control and switching the channel, I sat and watched as a physically fit woman around the same age as me started flashing her six-pack and flexing her muscles in places that I didn't even think possible. This woman was beyond buff. She was ripped. She was fit. And she certainly wasn't spending the majority of her time stuffing her face with a fresh bag of Cheetos. But in an effort to diffuse the situation—and to make me feel better about myself—my mind immediately went into defense mode. I began to compare myself to this woman, as destructive thoughts took over my brain and negativity quickly rolled into my mind. *She might be fit, but I bet she doesn't have three kids,* I thought. Followed by, *This woman gets paid to do this. If I got paid to work out, you had better believe I'd look like that, too.*

*Oh, I could totally do that . . . if I really wanted to,* I told myself.

And finally, *I wonder where this ad was filmed? That beach looks really pretty and very relaxing. I am so in need a vacation. What makes this woman so wonderful that she gets to be there while I'm stuck here?*

As nasty as those sentiments may sound, I couldn't stop myself from becoming envious of someone I didn't even know. No doubt I wanted to look like her; but more importantly, I wanted to *feel* like her . . . happy, fit, and healthy. But there I was—on the couch with a bag full of chips and a tube of chocolate chip cookie dough just waiting to be devoured. Even then, after watching this gal flaunt her stuff, my mind was continually reassuring me that I had no need for exercise. I was a mom of three kids after all, so what did I expect? Rather than motivating me to get off my posterior, my thoughts were holding me captive, keeping me stuck on my sofa and believing in the ridiculous excuses it kept coming up with . . . one after another.

But something was about to change.

In the exact moment my mind was busy comforting me, that same, muscle-clad woman—you know, the one who caused me such despair in the first place—had four . . . *yes, four!* of her young children now appearing next to her on this show. My mouth dropped open in astonishment. My excuses had officially expired and my mind only had one thing to say: *Well, girl . . . she's got you there.*

It was the truth. I'd reached the point where I couldn't justify my laziness anymore. I needed to change but wasn't exactly sure how to start or where to begin. I desired direction as to where to go and what to do. Scripture tells us that God will meet our needs when and where we need it most (Phil. 4:19). For me and in this instance, God met me on my couch, while engulfed in a full bag of chips, no less, and intervened through an infomercial of all things.

> *"Comparison is the thief of joy."*
>
> **—Theodore Roosevelt**

His goal was not to make me feel ashamed, nor compare myself to another, but He wanted me to shed those feelings of discontent and rid my heart of the negative feelings I was harboring inside. He knew how discouraged I was by the lack of attention I'd paid my own body over the past few years, and had decided it was finally time to get through to me, the only way I would listen.

Even if it was through the TV.

Yep. I had been awakened. I was ready for a change and eager for some muscle-tone to return again. I wanted to get healthy, and ditch those nasty habits for good. So, I put my tube of cookie dough down—after taking one last bite, of course—prayed for some strength, and made a plan to take some action.

This Wonder Woman Wannabe was headed to the gym . . . finally.

*But didn't my housework give me the exercise I need? Couldn't I just diet, instead? What if I got sucked up by one of those treadmills at the gym, causing my untimely death? What then?*

Ladies, you have now reached a "No Excuse" zone, which means the vast number of reasons you've come up with for not exercising are no longer valid from this point on. Believe me, I get it: we're busy. And for the years that our kiddos are still at home, our chaos is going to remain constant. It is our job to make an effort to implement a workout routine into our hectic schedules and around such craziness. This is where the challenge presents itself, but it's one that's totally doable and completely worth it. If I can do this, girls, then you can, too.

It's time to get started.

## PUMPING IT UP

Okay, so we've established that working out and becoming fit is of utmost importance as far as our overall physical well-being is concerned, but what we haven't figured out is how to implement an exercise program that will work for us, our schedules, and our budgets. Keep in mind that daily exercise is important, but if a trip to the gym three times a week isn't something that will work with your schedule and/or budget, then it's not the right routine for you. The most important thing here is finding an activity that will continually motivate you, one that you won't lose the desire to do.

As for me, well, prior to falling off the workout bandwagon, I had spent plenty of time in the gym setting. I was an intercollegiate athlete in the sport of softball back in my college days, so I knew what to lift and how to lift it in order to make muscles appear once again. I was aware of what cardio programs I liked to participate in, which ones worked for me, and those that just weren't my thing. But before you decide to sign up for a gym membership, or spend a ton of money on equipment or home workout programs, you'll want to take the time to do your research. Sit down and make a list of activities you enjoy, and check out all the programs in your area that will accommodate your fitness interests.

Here are some tips to consider when doing just that.

**Choose your style.** Exercising doesn't have to occur at a gym. You can devise a fitness routine of your own by using workout videos to guide you in your own home. Like the outdoors? Devise a workout regimen incorporating the elements outside. Honestly, there are a ton of options to choose from when selecting the right program. It really all comes down to where you are going to be the most comfortable, dedicated, and motivated.

**Establish a routine.** Figure out what you love to do whether it be running on the treadmill; swimming; or taking a spin, yoga, circuit training, or aerobics classes. Be willing to try new things, equipment, or maybe even set out to explore the weight rack. Remember, you aren't going to be a fan of every type of exercise out there, but by committing to at least trying some of them, you may just surprise yourself. Fair enough, right?

**Prepare a playlist.** In order to get really motivated, I need some good music to take the focus off of what I'm actually subjecting my body to. Gather up your favorite songs and use your iPod—or smartphone or even a Walkman with old-school cassettes—to play some of your favorite music at the gym. This helps immensely when attempting to fuel your desire to workout. It's also a great way to lift your mood and get your day headed in the right direction.

**Time for a trainer.** If you have no idea what you are doing at the gym, you are in luck. By booking an appointment with a staff trainer at your chosen facility, you'll receive the guidance you desire and that extra push you need. Trainers know how to get your body where you want it to be, but they can also be a bit pricey, too. Fortunately, most gyms offer a free training session to new members, so call around and see who's offering these types of incentives prior to joining.

### *Gym Gear*

Thankfully, the days of wearing leotards and other horrible '80s workout attire to the gym are long gone. Today it's about blending style and comfort. But have you looked at the prices of workout gear? Talk about expensive! To make it easy on yourself, and your purse, I recommend investing in just a few outfits to start off with. We're talking one pair of shoes, three sports bras, as well as three tops and bottoms you'll feel comfortable in. So, when you're out and about shopping for your fitness gear, keep a few of these tips in mind.

**Sports bras:** Believe me when I tell you that it's crucial to purchase the right size bra, ensuring that it's not too tight and that you're still able to breathe. I find this to be extremely helpful, especially when working out—the breathing I mean. You'll also want to make sure that you're getting enough support, guaranteeing that your breasts are completely covered and aren't in any danger of escaping . . . no matter how high you jump or how low you bend. Makes sense, right? Sports bras can also be pretty costly, though, so I suggest hitting up places such as TJ Maxx, Marshalls, Shopko, or other discounted clothing stores like these in order to score a sweet deal.

**Shoes:** Shoes can be really expensive . . . really, really expensive. Once again, try hitting up a discount store that sells athletic sneakers and attempt to get those puppies for a lot less. Make sure they fit, are comfortable, and are the right type of shoe for the exercise you will be committing to. When in doubt, ask a store salesman. You can also do a bit of your own research online by checking out reviews and other information on the shoes that interest you. Oh, and always try your shoes on *before* buying them. In fact, why not jump up and down, bust a few kicks, or maybe run a leisurely lap around the perimeter of the store to make sure that this investment is the right one for you. You'll be glad you did!

**Pants/shorts:** When it comes to work out attire, I have seen it all at the gym, ladies. So much so, that I feel the need to mention the fact that you should never wear materials such as denim, or wool—yes, I said wool!—to the gym. Besides, the clothes you work out in are supposed to be comfortable, right? So it's best to ask yourself these questions when shopping for your next pair of gym trunks: Will they absorb sweat? Can I move comfortably in them? Are they too short? Too long? Too loose? Too tight? Remember, not all workout pants are the same; so before purchasing, you'll want to try on each pair.

**T-shirts/tanks/tops:** I have to say that workout gear is super cute these days, and can actually invoke style in the midst of lifting barbells two feet above your head. But how stylish you want to look and how much you want to spend to do so is completely up to you. Remember, we are working out in an effort to become physically fit and healthy; so, purchase tees and tanks that will accommodate your workout, help you feel good in the process, and won't break the bank while you're at it.

**Hair and makeup**: Keep in mind that you are going to the gym to sweat—and sweat hard, I might add. You want your hair pulled back, and off of your face completely. As for makeup? Don't waste your time and money by putting this stuff on prior to a workout. Besides, we are there to impress no one except ourselves. Save the makeup for later . . . you know, when you're not covered in a vat of your own sweat.

**Deodorant:** Get one that works. I repeat: get one that works! There have been too many times at the gym where I've been stuck next to the person whose deodorant has failed them miserably. And I've become miserable because of it. Needless to say, don't be the stinky girl at the gym—apply your deodorant liberally in an effort to keep your body odor at bay . . . at least for an hour or two.

### *Mind and Motivation*

Okay, so now that you've got a feel for the type of exercise(s) you'd like to start out with and have the basics as far as apparel goes, here's a few more tidbits of advice to help get you out the door and on your way to a healthier, more wondrous you.

**Initiate body blinders.** When visiting a gym, girls, there's one thing you're going to want to keep in mind: comparison is the big, bad burglar of our happiness. I mention this again because it's easy to get swept up into wanting to look like the trainer, the aerobics instructor, or anyone else sporting a fit body. Remember that you are at the gym to become a better steward of your own body, not fall victim to poor self-esteem based off what others may look like. Now, I know you already know this, but even as Christian women who know better than to let such things bother them, we also happen to be human and can struggle in this area. Put on your blinders, focus on *your* body, and let the rest take care of itself.

**Bring a friend.** Nothing says BFFs like a mean workout routine you both can participate in. I can honestly say that some of the best times spent at the gym (yes, I just uttered those words in the same sentence) have occurred while exercising with friends. By bringing an ally, you are more likely to be motivated to keep your dates with the gym—and stick to your workout routine. It's one of the best things you can do for your psyche, for fun, and for your overall health.

**Start slow.** You can't expect to just jump into exercising and run five miles on your first day of your new workout program. Understand that you have to ease into your workout routine. Start off slow and build from there. Your body, and your muscles, will thank you for it.

**Create incentives.** Every girl needs some motivation, right? Well, for me, there's nothing like receiving a reward for my hard work in the gym. Maybe it's a new purse or a new pair of shoes? Or maybe, it's a triple scoop sundae with all of the fixings from my favorite ice cream shop. Whatever your personal enticement might be, fix your eyes upon it and then set out to achieve it. There's nothing wrong with a little incentive to help fuel your motivation.

**Enjoy the endorphins.** On top of all of the other benefits of working out, here's one more: our bodies release chemicals known as endorphins that can actually be mood enhancers. No, really! In case you didn't already know about this, the release of endorphins is a great way to give a boost to your mental health. Hey, I need help anywhere I can get it, so if I can shed a few pounds, gain some muscle where flab used to be, and get rid of some stress in the process—bring it on!

**Don't get discouraged.** Getting physically fit isn't an easy process by any means and requires a lot of hard work and determination on your part. At times, it can be discouraging when the results you *want* seem to take forever to *get*. Stay the course, girls, don't give up, and remember that the end result you're striving for is so worth the effort you're putting into it. You can do this!

16

# Donning Mom Jeans: When Mama Needs a Makeover

*"If the waistband of your jeans could double as a push-up bra or your backside looks flatter than a flapjack, you're guilty of wearing 'Mom Jeans.' These high-waisted horrors are cardinal sins of fashion."*

**—Stacy London,** ***What Not to Wear***

I swore it would never happen to me. I made a promise to myself—and to that hip, young teenager I once was—that no matter how old I got and how many children I brought into this world, I was never (as in ever), going to ditch my desires to remain fashionable. You see, once upon a time and way back when, I had visions of becoming a trendy mom, you know—the type of mama that just oozed style? Yep. I had intentions of wearing the coolest fashions, the hippest hairdos, and keeping up-to-date with the most popular threads . . . well, as long as they no longer included teased hair and acid washed jeans.

But without realizing it, my fashion sense began a steady decline after my introduction to motherhood occurred just ten short years ago. You see, somehow, those notorious "Mom jeans" managed to find their way into my closet—you know, the unflattering, pleated, baggy, denim pants that sit directly south of one's breasts. A minivan, the same one we discussed in Chapter Two, also appeared in my driveway. And unbeknownst to me, grey hairs began emerging where my brunette locks once dominated . . . strand after silvery strand of them.

Wonder Woman doesn't get gray hair. She doesn't don Mom jeans, either. And as we've explored previously, she certainly doesn't drive a minivan. But this Wannabe (pointing finger at self), this one apparently does.

Superhero wannabe or not, I was painfully aware of the fact that I had grown into the woman my sixteen-year-old self would have developed reoccurring nightmares over. I had become a mom in desperate need of a makeover, and let's be honest here, a complete fashion overhaul. This mama was in need of some serious help.

We're talking a fashion emergency of sorts.

But, as I stared at my reflection in the mirror, I couldn't help but feel confused by the inner workings of my brain. Don't worry, this happens often. As I stood there, my hands perched upon the spot where my waist used to exist, I couldn't help but think, *Do I really need to be consumed with my outward appearance? Is that what's really important?*

The teenager within was desperately trying to claw her way out in an effort to scream, "Yes!" But the twenty- . . . thirty-five-year-old woman looking back at me couldn't help but remain puzzled. I mean, as a Christian mom, why would I be worried about such a thing? Why would I care about my exterior as long as my interior was spiritually sound? After all, that's what was most important here, wasn't it . . . and that's when Peter came to mind:

> *"Your beauty should not come from outward adornment, such as elaborate hairstyles and the wearing of gold jewelry or fine clothes. Rather, it should be that of your inner self, the unfading beauty of a gentle and quiet spirit, which is of great worth in God's sight."*
>
> **—1 Peter 3:3–4**

Followed by a "shout-out" from Paul:

> *"Likewise also that women should adorn themselves in respectable apparel, with modesty and self-control, not with braided hair and gold or pearls or costly attire."*
>
> **—1 Timothy 2:9 ESV**

This is when my confusion hit an all-time high, guilt officially set in, and I had no clue as to whether or not I should donate all of my clothes to charity—and resolve to wearing nothing but housecoats and slippers for the rest of my life—or if a different, less drastic path was warranted.

The answer was yes . . . and no . . . and maybe so. Do they even still make housecoats?

## THE CHRISTIAN COMPLEX

Now, I have to admit that I struggled a little bit when ultimately deciding to write this chapter. I didn't want to distract from the importance of our inner selves by focusing on outdated outer appearances, of all things. Obviously, the state of our "insides" and the spiritual path we're headed on is so much more important than what we're sporting externally, which led me back to the same question: As Christian mothers, should our wardrobes really matter? And if so, why?

Let me attempt to shed some light on this topic.

As we've begun to age, our priorities with our wardrobe—and maybe even our fashion sense in general—has seemingly decreased in significance. We're lucky if we can locate clean, coordinating clothes that don't have any residual formula, boogers, or other unidentified fluids still lurking on them. To us, uncontaminated, crust-free apparel equates to a successful outfit. But as a mom who spends most of her time tending to others, I have to admit that I desire something more than this. For me, my goals with clothing simply consist of dressing nicely and in a way that correctly fits my body type. I want comfortable clothes that I'm able to feel good in. And I want a wardrobe that will allow me to express who I am on the inside, as well as my role as a church-going mommy and wife on the outside. I've got impressionable, young kiddos to look out for, which means I have to stress the importance of modesty—in a present-day culture that screams anything but.

So, you see, this chapter isn't about focusing on designer labels, or celebrity-endorsed apparel. This section is all about dressing to bring out the Wonder Woman inside of you. It's about wearing on the outside what you're feeling on the inside in a positive, modest, and appropriate way. It's about bringing your personality out and reclaiming your individuality as a woman and a mom. We're not defying what the Bible says, nor what Peter or Timothy divulges; rather, we're allowing our interiors to finally match our exteriors.

*Wow!* I think I just wrote a battle cry of sorts.

Please understand my certainty when I say that dressing fashionably and practicing our Christian values *can* coexist as long as the former doesn't take precedence over the latter. We can dress sleek. We can be chic. We can have a haircut with some style. We can even wear jewelry . . . and we don't have to feel guilty about it as long as we've got our priorities straight. Fashion should never be our focus, but Mom jeans should never have to grace our bodies either.

So, let's figure out how to get you looking snazzy by means of clothing, hair, and makeup, all while implementing a budget at the same time. Sounds good, right? I thought so, too. Let's figure this out together.

### *Tip #1: Mama Gets a Dress Code.*

*Ahem.* It's confession time.

As it turns out, modesty was *not* my middle name as a young adult. The idea of discretion was not a value I practiced as far as my style of dress was concerned back in the day. My wardrobe mostly consisted of items that were way too short, a bit too tight, and fairly suggestive. Midriff shirts, crop tops, and even short shorts were all garments I wore to school and other social events without a second thought. Are you gasping yet? In my defense, I wasn't a church-going gal at the time, and the idea of even considering modesty never really crossed my mind. As far as I knew, what I was wearing was more than acceptable and the attention I gained because of it was something I embraced.

Are you cringing as much as I am right now?

Today is a much different story. As a Christian mother of three, I'm obligated to dress in a modest manner and teach the same lesson to my children. I'm required to lead by example, because whether we moms realize it or not, our kiddos are always—and I mean, always—watching our every move. It's as if we're on a surveillance camera around the clock, isn't it? They mimic our mannerisms, replicate our speech, and become miniature versions of ourselves. So much so that if we expect them to listen when we preach modesty to our children, then as their mothers, we must set the bar high as far as our own standards of dress go. We certainly can't be telling our youngsters one thing and then doing another.

So, what's a mom to do . . . and what should she wear?

Dannah Gresh, author of the best-selling Secret Keeper Girl Series, uses a great tool that we moms, and our young daughters, can adopt into our way of dress and selected style. Remember, as moms, we want to look great, stay comfortable, and outfit ourselves in a way that won't display everything God gave us. The guidelines can be extremely helpful when dressing each morning, as well as when purchasing new clothes. It's called the "Truth or Bare Fashion Test," and goes a little something like this:

**The "raise and praise" test:** Reach for the sky! No, really . . . try it. This is the perfect opportunity early in the morning to see if that shirt you're sporting is too short for your own good. Better to test it at home than in public, I say. Once you've got those arms reaching high, look down to see if your navel is exposed—or any other part of your tummy. Depending on your findings, you may want to pitch it and plan on investing in something with a little more length next time, instead.

**The "mirror, mirror" test:** If you're donning shorts or a skirt, then you must try this exercise before heading out the door. Using a chair (a toilet works great too), sit down in front of your mirror. What do you see? If your legs are crossed and your shorts or skirt appear to still be at an appropriate level, then you are good to go. But if your underwear is staring back at you, or if the waistband of your skirt or pants are sinking dangerously low (how is that even comfortable?), then head back into your closet and select something a bit more appropriate and a lot less revealing. Simple enough, right?

**The "I see London, I see France" test:** I might see London and I might even see France, but I definitely don't want to see your underpants. Can I just state for the record that showing your underwear in public will never become a popular fashion statement, ever? Bend over and touch your toes . . . or just slump over like I do. Can you see through your pants? Are your underwear lines showing through? Can another person tell that you have your granny bloomers on today instead of your briefs? If you answered yes to any one of these questions, then your pants may be a little too snug. Make your way back to the armoire and select a different item. Repeat test as necessary.

**The "over and out" test**: Peek-a-boo, I don't want to see you. Hey, God gave us breasts for a reason, but it certainly wasn't so we could wear low-cut shirts and let them hang out, now was it? Besides, after having three children, "hanging" is about all mine do these days (and no one wants to see that). So, if you're unsure whether you fall into this category, bend down into a hanging position and look into the mirror. When you bend over, do your breasts go on display? If so, it looks like it's time to purchase a new shirt and toss out the one you just had on. This is especially true if you're headed out to a PTA meeting, or on your way to church. Keep those girls covered up!

**The "Spring Valley" test:** Accentuating one's figure is one thing, but wearing clothes that restrict breathing is another. If your heart is racing, your respiration is labored, and your shirt or pants feel so tight that you fear you may just pass out, then it looks like it's time for some new duds. Remember, we want to be comfortable, classy, and tasteful in what we're wearing. Items that shift and contort our bodies into different shapes are not the look, or the feel, we girls should be shooting for.

This bodes true when trying on clothes in the dressing rooms as well. I mean, have you ever had an instance where you *may* have inadvertently tried on an article of clothing one size too small, and then spent a good twenty minutes trying to free yourself from it? I've found myself in this exact predicament, half-panicked, and worried that the sales clerk . . . or an emergency first responder . . . would be required in order to set me free. But incidents like these have made me realize that if a garment looks like it's too tight on the hanger, chances are, it's going to be *way* too tight on my body. Rule of thumb: tight-fitting clothes are overrated—choose comfortable yet classy and you'll never go wrong.

### *Tip #2: Just Because It Zips, Doesn't Mean It Fits.*

I think it's safe to say that the majority of us moms could be found guilty of a serious fashion no-no on one occasion or another, whether we've meant to do so or not. As admitted earlier, I've worn plenty of garments in the past that didn't necessarily jive with the definition of modesty . . . items that should never have been made in the first place, let alone worn in public for others to see. It's evident that at times, we girls can go through episodes where our judgment and overall sense of style may come into question. Times when we may have thought it a good idea, for example, to purchase and wear mint green hi-tops, of all things. Moments where we voluntarily made the decision to fully embrace the shoulder pad movement by placing them in every shirt, blouse, or jacket we owned. Oh, and who could forget all of the times where we've contemplated throwing on those Wonder Woman Underoos of old and running through the sprinklers in the front yard—not caring whether the neighbors deemed us slightly deranged? Okay, maybe that last example was directed more toward me, but you get the idea. Either way, it's in memorable fashion moments such as these that we need to consider the following in what not to wear . . . and just say no.

### What Not to Wear—Wannabe Style

**Stay out of the Juniors section.** Look down below. See the area right in between your waist and your woman parts? Ladies, those are your hips, and once we've got those we can kiss any effort to dress in the Juniors section good-bye. Yes, girls, once we've hit a certain age—the stage of our lives where our hips have expanded—we've got to realize that any desire to visit this portion of the department store should be reconsidered. We're women! We've had kids! And the type of clothing housed in these sections just weren't made with us in mind. Instead, they were geared toward the younger set . . . much, much younger in fact. Hence the name Juniors. So, as a rule, if you find yourself contemplating whether or not to buy the cute shorts and trendy little top featured on a pre-pubescent mannequin, by all means put it back. Do not pass "Go." Do not collect $200. Simply hang those items back on the rack and proceed to the nearest exit. Like, immediately. We're women and we need to choose items that are meant to accommodate our figures. Amen?!

**Bags are for carrying, not wearing.** Another general rule when it comes to selecting items for your wardrobe is that in no way, shape, or form should your style of dress resemble a bag. Not sure what I mean? Whether it be plastic, brown, or environmentally friendly, bags are for shopping with, not for wearing. "Baggy" is not a desired look, nor is it a trend we want anything to do with. Here's a rule to follow: if it hangs off of you, then it needs to be left hanging in the store . . . not placed in your closet.

**Get out of the closet.** If you've ever had the desire to raid your daughter's closet in an attempt to borrow her clothing, resist! This can be considered even worse than shopping in the Juniors section. Word to the wise: turn around, walk out of her room, and figure out a better solution. Seriously!

**It's so hard to say good-bye.** I have some articles of clothing that I absolutely love. Unfortunately, these same items are so old they can practically be considered vintage. They're frayed around the edges and are so worn out from use that their material has almost become see-through. Every article of clothing reaches a point where it has to be donated or thrown away. We ladies need to know when it's time to bid adieu, practice cleaning out our closets regularly, and then hit the mall for some new apparel.

### *Tip #3: Shopping 101: Resolving Issues*

Many moms flat-out detest the mere thought of shopping, let alone actually partaking in it. Maybe it's the horrible store lighting, the small confines of those dressing rooms, or the awkward moment when the sales clerk checks on you only to ask if you'll be needing a bigger size. Yes, all of these reasons and more can make us girls fed up with the whole process—and contribute to giving us a major complex, too. But it's time to address these problems, figure out how to handle them, and move on from the nightmares associated with finding new clothes. Got an issue? I think I've got you covered!

### First Issue: "I don't know how to dress my body."

Learning how to dress your body by figuring out what types of cuts and lengths are most flattering to your figure can be a bit tricky. In fact, nine times out of ten, the items displayed on the malnourished mannequin in the department store have never looked as good on me as they did on her. The trick, my friends, is figuring out the best type of fit for our bodies, and finding items we can be comfortable in.

By using your favorite search engine, you can locate online Web sites like shopyourshape.com. Sites such as these offer instruction to help you identify your body shape, and then provide a tutorial on what garments you should be looking for on your next shopping trip. Some even provide great suggestions on items you can purchase directly through their Web sites as well. Gotta love that!

### Second Issue: "I have no idea how to coordinate clothes."

Coordinating clothes can be difficult, especially when styles and trends seem to be changing constantly. Thankfully, we have the Internet to help us ladies figure out our wardrobe issues, all in the comfort of our own homes. By visiting helpful sites like polyvore.com, you'll be amazed by what you can put together, the types of colors you can add to your wardrobe, as well as what kinds of accessories will best coordinate with the clothes you select. Even better, you can peruse outfits that other guests have matched together, or make up a collection all your own. *And* if this wasn't awesome enough, polyvore.com will tell you exactly where to find the item(s) you're wanting and provide you with the retail price, as well. Ahh, efficiency at its best!

### Third Issue: "I'm on a tight budget."

Aren't we all these days? Hey, we have kids to feed, a mortgage to pay, and recurring bills that keep finding their way into our mailboxes. A new wardrobe may not be in the budget unless we can find items that not only look great, but don't cost a lot, either. If you're budget is slim, try incorporating some of these tips to help.

**Hit up the sales.** I'm a sucker for a good sale and nothing makes me feel better than leaving a store with great items in hand and a receipt confirming the fact that I just saved more money than I actually spent. By taking advantage of sales—usually around each and every holiday—you can save big . . . as in huge. Oh, and word to the wise: pre-holiday sales are most definitely the time to stock up on clothes and get some shopping done.

**Buy post-season.** Each season of the year brings a whole new line of clothing for retail stores. What does this mean for you? Huge savings of course! By planning your shopping trips around the end of a fashion season, you may encounter deals in excess of 75 percent off of regularly priced merchandise. This keeps a lot more money in your wallet and a lot less room in your closet.

**Use coupons.** Most major retailers have Web sites and/or use social media outlets to promote their stores and offer their customers significant savings. Find these sites, "like" their Facebook pages, and you'll be able to keep up with all of the super sales they're advertising throughout the year. In addition, subscribe to your newspaper and get on your selected stores' mailing lists to ensure you don't miss out on a thing—like all of those great coupons they send out. This is a great way to save additional money, usually on top of already reduced prices. *Cha-ching!*

**Buy used.** Once you know what styles look great for your body type, try visiting a consignment store while out and about. You can usually score some slightly used but great finds for a phenomenal price. If you haven't shopped consignment as of yet, use your local directory and pay a visit to one soon. You may just find something you can't live without.

All right, so hopefully you've gotten a better idea as to what you should be wearing, understand what you should never put on, and kind of get the gist of how to buy great clothes for a lot less money. But what about your hair? How about your makeup? These are two areas that we must also address if we're going to further our discussion on mommy makeovers. So what do you say we start chatting about our hair . . . and the makeup we wear?

### *Tip #4: Hairstyles Gone Wrong: Don't Try This at Home!*

Oh, how hairstyles change, don't they? Whether you choose to wear your hair length short, medium, or long, there's no denying that your hairstyle has probably undergone some major changes with the passing of each new decade. Some eras were good to us, while others (can you say the '80s?) had us donning styles that were anything but flattering, and sometimes just downright weird. In fact, take a moment to look at your senior portrait from high school. Now, look at your mom's. And your grandmother's. Chances are, the hairstyles displayed in each one of these images are dramatically different. Trends change and fads fade, but I think it's safe to say that as one decade passes and moves into another, so should our hairstyles.

What worked for us as teenagers is probably not the ideal cut for us now. As busy mamas, most of us are in search of a hairdo that will keep us looking hip and fresh, and one that will also work with our current lifestyle. Many of us aren't sure how to select a hairstyle that will best suit our features, which usually has us flipping through magazines, and choosing a celebrity coif we'd like to achieve, instead. Speaking from experience though, all previous attempts of trying to reproduce a star-status hairstyle have failed me miserably. I've actually left a salon sporting a haircut that was so bad—we're talking a modern-day mullet here—that I couldn't help but break down and cry. Does it sound trivial? Absolutely. But when you're sporting a freshly shorn mullet, you realize how bad a bad haircut can be.

But all of this can be avoided (*phew!*) by visiting Web sites like thehairstyler.com and entering all sorts of information about your facial structure, complexion, age, and the desired look of your hair. This site and others like it will provide you with the type of cut that will best enhance your features and take the guess-work out of the equation. Prior to your next trip to the salon, give it a try and see what you come up with. It may just be your best cut yet.

Now, even though we have the tools in front of us these days to ensure a great cut and style, sometimes things can still go horribly wrong. Yep. Sometimes we choose to follow certain trends or opt for styles that may not be the best suit for us. In order to help, I've provided a short list of hairstyles that should probably be avoided—like the plague. Feel free to read on and if you're still rocking any one of these styles, it may be time for a new do for you:

- ☆ If the sides of your hair are very short, but that back of your hair is extremely long (yes, I'm referring to a mullet), don't walk to the hair salon . . . RUN!
- ☆ If your bangs are stacked upon your forehead and require half a bottle of hairspray in order to secure them there, you are in need of a new hairstyle . . . and maybe a deep conditioning treatment, as well.

- ☆ If the side of your hair is fanned out and you look as though you could pick up a synthesizer and bust the '80s classic, "I Ran," by Flock of Seagulls, this is an indication that it is time for a change.
- ☆ If your hair is beginning to gray (when you see one, it means more are on their way), you have two options. If you'd like to hide said invaders, either visit the grocery store for some quick color or make an appointment with a reputable hair salon. Or, if you're digging the distinguished look, let those silver locks grow—embrace it.
- ☆ If you're thinking it's time for a change, and decide that you have yet to don a Mohawk, please re-read this chapter, and then enlist the help of a hairstylist in order to avoid anything too trendy.
- ☆ If you're thinking that your hairstyle from 1990 will eventually come back into fashion in another ten years or so, just like your wardrobe might, you're probably right . . . but that doesn't mean you should wait that long to change your hairstyle. Update your look now.

And finally, no matter what you decide to do with your hairstyle, remember that hair is just that: hair! What matters the most is what you feel comfortable with and what works best for both you and your lifestyle. Hey, I get it, and your hairstylist should, too. If you're feeling like a change, and don't have a hair salon that you visit regularly, seek out a friend's recommendation.

A new hairdo can make all the difference for a style that may be fading, or lacking in some other way, shape, or form. Use the tips I suggested and let the trained professionals assist you by keeping your locks updated, chic, and oh-so-sleek.

## *Tip #5: Less Is More: Makeup Magic*

Just like hairstyles, we've also seen a lot of changes in the world of cosmetics over the past six thousand years or so. No, really; women, and sometimes even men, have been painting their faces since long before Christ came to save us. Whether they stained their lips with berries or used other natural elements to alter their looks, the practice of applying makeup goes way back in history. Luckily, we no longer have to retreat outdoors in an effort to locate berries in order to get some color on our lips. Nope. These days, we have an endless supply of choices. And like anything that provides us with a surplus of options, it can be hard for us to choose. But here's some advice to consider the next time you want to change out your cosmetics bag:

**Visit a professional.** Make an appointment with a makeup artist in order to find colors that will best accentuate your face, hair, and complexion. You'll also be given the opportunity to learn useful techniques, and tricks on how to apply your makeup in a timely manner, and without a lot of effort.

**Check out the Internet.** Use your uber-handy search engine and explore the Internet for up-to-date tips and techniques. Virtually every cosmetics company has a Web site loaded with tutorials on how to apply their products, as well as useful info regarding the selection of colors. Magazines and Web sites dedicated to style often serve as great resources on the latest looks and finding the best brand of makeup for you.

**Avoid the trends**. Let's face it: makeup is expensive and investing in trendy colors—you know, like purple, teal, and green eyeliner that will undoubtedly be deemed outdated by next season—just isn't worth it. As moms, we should probably opt for a more natural look as opposed to one that screams, "I miss the '80s and am so glad they're bringing those colors back." Know what I mean? Ladies, you need to be able to spot trends and not waste your hard-earned money on them.

Go with neutral tones that accentuate your already-fabulous features. Just sayin'!

**Always wear sunscreen**. I'm fair-complected, which means my skin is usually a lighter shade of pale—or redder than red after subjecting it to the sun. Make sure to protect yourself each and every day by wearing sunscreen as a base coat *under* your makeup. Even though most foundations on the market today already contain sunscreen in them, I would suggest taking this a step further by doubling up for added protection. Girls, it doesn't matter what season it is or whether the sun is out or not. Using sunscreen each and every day to prevent premature aging, sun damage, and yes, skin cancer, is a must. Put it on now and you won't be sorry later. Capisce?

**Invest in skin care**. Friends, when it comes to preserving our skin and fighting the signs of aging, investing in a good skin care line is a smart play. When I was about twenty-seven years old, I noticed something a bit strange in a picture taken of me right after the birth of my son. Rather than focusing on the image of that sweet baby in my arms, I was fixated on the skin surrounding my eye instead. It looked as if a bird had literally taken its foot and stepped right on the side of my face. I had wrinkles!!! And no matter how hard I tried to wipe them off, no superhuman amount of strength was going to get rid of them. Nope, those pleats of skin were there for good! Unfortunately, it appeared that my skin was prematurely wrinkling and the time to perform damage control had arrived. By investing in a line of skin care products, my sole intention wasn't only to combat Mother Nature and Father Time, but to also rid my skin of the daily pollutants it was battling. Girls, let me just say that taking care of our skin is important and it's never too late . . . or early to start. Seriously.

Wow, we've certainly covered a lot of material in this chapter, huh? But as I stated before, and what I firmly believe, is that this portion of the book was written to help not harm. By no means do I think all of us moms are in need of makeovers, nor do I feel that our external appearance is of utmost importance. The information relayed here is meant to provide you with tips and advice, but I am not suggesting that you *need* to improve yourself; rather, I've written it just in case you *want* to.

*Phew!* So glad I got that disclaimer out there. Now let's move on to the next chapter of the book already, shall we?

# 17

# THE WANNABE'S TOTIN' A HUGE HANDBAG

*"The number of useless items (and trinkets) a mother's purse holds for her children quite possibly defies the law(s) of physics . . . and gravity."*

**—The Wannabe**

Gosh, if there's one thing we moms have a lot of these days, it's got to be an overabundance of "stuff." It fills up our cars, our homes . . . and especially those handbags we're forced to carry. Indeed, our purses have seemingly become magnets for lost trinkets, unexplained junk, and loads of other useless items that can't help but make us wonder how they got there in the first place. Chances are, if you're a purse-toting mom like me, you've found yourself bombarded by the overwhelming contents of your oversized handbag on more than one occasion.

*Geesh!* If only we got paid by the pound for the contents of our handbags, right? If only someone would willingly give us cash for the most haphazard items within our bags, it might all be worth it. Let's just say, as a mom with a slew of randomness residing in her purse, it wouldn't be the first time I had hoped for something so foolish. But the producers from *Let's Make a Deal* aren't banging down my door looking for the next Wonder Woman-clad contestant whose junked-out purse is worthy enough to be awarded money.

Unfortunately for the mainstream population of moms out there, the clutter and chaos we've got going on within those satchels of ours merely suggests we're in need of some re-organization—and maybe a large dumpster parked outside to help get rid of the mess.

Just how bad could it be you ask? Take a look for yourself. After rummaging through my own purse, here's a list of the contents I recently discovered:

- ☆ Over twenty crumpled receipts from the grocery store, the dry cleaners, and my most recent trip to the mall.
- ☆ Three die-cast metal cars—of course, I have boys.
- ☆ Spiderman's nemesis.
- ☆ A pair of cheap sunglasses with one lens totally missing—there went $20.00.
- ☆ A smartphone charger cord found strangling my wallet, almost to death.
- ☆ A tampon, recently escaped from its wrapper, broken in two, and no longer deemed useable.
- ☆ One maxi pad whose "wings" have spread and are now trapping dirt, debris, and all the other residue found at the bottom of my purse.
- ☆ My wallet—as I said, just barely alive.
- ☆ One toddler-sized sock—its mate? MIA.
- ☆ Three Dora the Explorer stickers (???).
- ☆ A half-eaten granola bar along with all of its crumbs.
- ☆ An old lollipop, previously sucked on, half-eaten and covered in unidentified objects.
- ☆ Nine week's worth of sermons notes from church.

- One diaper in a size way too small for my toddler.
- One pacifier clip-on device. (Hmm . . . my kid never used a pacifier past one week of age. He's three now. Not sure what's going on here).
- Sand, yes, sand, and I live nowhere near a beach.
- A Slinky. (C'mon, doesn't everyone have a Slinky in their purse?)
- A bouncy ball—these should be eradicated from every doctor's office kiddie reward chest on the planet (or at least in my town).
- One pair of toddler underwear, just in case.
- One opened and empty tube of anti-bacterial gel. (Can you guess where I found the rest of it?)
- One bag of travel wipes, opened and completely dried out . . . gee, that's helpful.

With all this junk taking up valuable space within my purse, it's no wonder I can't find important items when I need them. It shouldn't be a surprise at the grocer's checkout line when I struggle to locate the whereabouts of my rewards card, but can instantly produce a tampon instead . . . and accidentally whip it out of my purse as means of payment. Yes, it's quite obvious that I've got way too much junk going on and that it might be time to do something about it—before it sends me over the edge for good.

Tell me you can relate?

## HANDBAG INTERVENTION

Before becoming a mom, handbag mayhem was never even an issue. Way back when, I was a fairly organized girl with a desire to accessorize and a fetish for cute purses. I could have cared less how functional they were—all that mattered at that time was how well they helped accentuate my outfit. No, seriously; my purse collection was not to be outdone and consisted of short ones, fat ones, tall ones, thin ones, multicolored ones, purses with bows, purses with bling, clutch purses . . . and the list went on and on.

But that was a long time ago.

These days, my "collection" consists of nothing more than three (!) of the largest purses you have ever seen in your entire life. They might actually be constituted as hip trash bags. Not only do they lug all of my junk around, but they are so large, sturdy, and unbelievably spacious that my three-year-old could quite possibly ride in one of them, if so inclined. And you know what happens when you have a huge purse? You guessed it—a million different objects find their way into it, and pretty soon, your handbag has become a wasteland for useless items. Purses like mine should be off-limits to people like me: a purse-junkie guilty of carrying and hoarding rubbish, and using her handbag to do so.

Sounds like I need an intervention of sorts. Maybe you do, too.

So, what should we do? How do we get our satchels under control and avoid being swallowed (whole) by the confines of our handbags? Check out these tips to get that purse of yours clean, organized, and functional.

**Go smaller.** Rather than having a bag that could house a small village, try opting for one that's a bit smaller. Bigger isn't always better.

**Clean your clutch.** Remember way back in Chapter Two, when we discussed organizing and routinely cleaning your car on the fifteenth of each month? That also happens to be the perfect time to clean out that purse of yours. Make it sparkle!

**Stock it.** You need only stock your purse with the necessary essentials. Nothing more, nothing less.

**Pick a pocket.** Designate pockets in your purse for specific items/essentials you will need to carry. For example, your cell phone should be contained in the same compartment each and every time. Assign a spot for your wallet as well. Be consistent with where you store your necessities within the confines of your bag. Doing so will help keep your purse organized in between cleanings and won't have you scrambling to find things. Makes sense, right?

**Mama's got a brand new bag.** If your current purse is no longer working for you—or has been to war and has the battle scars to prove it—looks like it's time to invest in a new one. In fact, you may even want to replace your purses annually, or at least just prior to them becoming ripped, battered, bruised, and torn to shreds. Remember, you're looking for function mixed with style and will want to select a bag possessing the components you need. Be picky, take your time; and while some people luck out and stumble upon the perfect find at a thrift store, don't be afraid to spend a little bit of money in order to get a purse that will work for you and your needs.

## STOCKING OUR SATCHELS

Based off of the contents I just shared in my own purse, you are now aware of what *not* to place in your own. Instead, equip your handbags with the essential daily components that being a busy mom requires. Here are a few of the basics you should consider carrying at all times.

**Wallet:** I find this to be a really helpful item to have on hand, especially when wanting to purchase something. Crazy, I know.

**Tiny emergency kit:** We're talking about a few sterile bandages, some ointment, and a small tube of sunscreen in a sealed plastic bag, and stored in one of those convenient compartments within your purse.

**Baby wipes:** Very important and very necessary. Whether you have small children or big ones, you will always need a pack of these on hand.

**Headache relief:** I always find that when I'm shopping with my ten-year-old daughter, Ibuprofen or Tylenol really comes in handy and might be a good idea to carry in your purse. Disclaimer: If you have small children, make sure it is kept hidden, zipped, and unable to be tampered with. Oh, and consult your doctor before using any medication.

**Cell phone:** As you well know, this is a necessity. Never leave home without it. Ever.

**Feminine needs**: It's unsafe and of no use to you when the feminine hygiene items you're desperately in need of have found their way out of their packages and into the mainstream portion of your purse. You'll want to make sure to keep all protection hidden safely in a designated compartment of your purse—and ideally away from your wallet. This will ensure that mishaps don't occur and emergency hygiene situations don't become paramount.

**Back-up diapers**: If you're children are older, then this doesn't apply to you at all. But if you've got wee ones, then by all means place two extra diapers or training pants (in the correct size) in a pocket of your purse. Blowouts happen, and you'll need to be prepared when they do.

**Breath fresheners:** We all need these from time to time, but as I have found, if they're not hidden within my handbag, my children will consume them long before I get the opportunity to freshen my breath. If you're a big coffee drinker, store an ample supply at all times and keep them away from your offspring.

**Coupons!:** Many of us use coupons (as discussed in Chapter Twelve) and most of us would benefit from keeping an organizer in our purses to contain those clippings. I can't tell you how many times I've gone to a store only to have forgotten my invaluable vouchers at home. No doubt it's infuriating, but this problem can be resolved by keeping your coupons in your purse and with you at all times.

**Etc.:** Hey, it's your purse; and even though the supplies I mentioned can be helpful, ultimately it's your choice. You need to customize your bag with your specific needs. Keep in mind, you'll want to select items that will continue your quest toward making you a prepared mama, without weighing you down. Just remember that less is more when it comes to stocking your purse(s). Pick your items accordingly.

## SO MANY BAGS . . . SO LITTLE TIME?

There are still a few moms out there who possess a collection—as in more than three—handbags and love to accessorize with them no matter how busy their lives might be. You girls are the "fashionistas" of the group and love to color-coordinate your bags and outfits. I get it. It's an expression of sorts, and if this sounds like you—and I understand because it was once me—then you have a trickier task in front of you. I say this because you'll need to switch out purses, and the contents of them, more frequently. You must also remember to stock each of your individual bags with the necessary items I've outlined above, all while attempting to be more organized in your efforts when doing so. If up to the challenge, you may want to follow some of these additional tips.

**Stock up.** Include the same essential items in each of your purses. You know—items that we chatted about before and things you *need* to have in case of a minor emergency while out shopping.

**Store 'em.** Store your purses in the same area of your closet. Hang them up and switch them out as often as necessary. Being mindful of organization is key.

**Clean 'em.** All of your purses should probably undergo a thorough cleaning at least every other month. If using a rotation of handbags, realize that this will take up a bit more of your time; but honestly, having each of your purses stocked and ready to go with the items you'll need is so worth it.

Girls, remember, a purse needs to be much more than just a cute accessory these days. Whether you've got one pocketbook or an infinite supply of them, take time to ensure each one is properly stocked and somewhat organized before you step foot out of that door each morning.

This will eliminate a lot of the stress associated with having too much clutter and not enough necessities within your reach.

And finally, when purchasing your next purse, keep in mind that bigger isn't necessarily better, just as "cute" doesn't necessarily trump "practical." Your selection must be able to house the essentials you need in an organized, controlled fashion. Sure, your purse needs to be aesthetically pleasing, but more importantly, your purse needs to be extraordinarily functional.

# 18

# ADVENTURES IN GOING SOLO (NO, REALLY!)

*"By and large, mothers and housewives are the only workers who do not have regular time off. They are the great vacationless class."*

**—Anne Morrow Lindbergh**

You did it. And even though you're not exactly sure how it all came about, you've managed to exit your home without the usual entourage in tow. You're going solo, which means there's no screaming, no begging, and absolutely no one else vying for your attention—at this time. You are alone . . . and it's at this point that you've realized you have absolutely no idea as to what to do with yourself. Backing out of the driveway—in the minivan, no less—the only decision you're forced to make is whether you should sing aloud to your favorite iPod tunes, as opposed to the Veggie Tales CD that's been on the repeat function for the past two months, or indulge in the sweet sound of silence that fills your ears instead—not to mention an occasional complete thought or two. You've got a few hours all to yourself, which leaves you scrambling to figure out just how to put this valuable time to good use.

"I should go to the mall. I really do need some new shoes," you think aloud.

"Ooh, what about the day spa? A massage would be utterly amazing right now. I sooooo need a massage!" you exclaim.

"Oh but wait, my driver's license is about to expire; I should probably get to the DMV and take care of it." Responsibility rears its ugly head again. "Ugh, the DMV is the last place I want to spend my free time!"

Sure, you've got options, and since you're on your own that means the possibilities are endless as to how you're going to choose to spend your time. But you'd better make up your mind quick, because that sweet hubby of yours has only offered to take your offspring for a few, short hours, and the stopwatch on your free time has officially begun.

Yep. The countdown is on . . . so what are *you* going to do?

## TIME FLIES WHEN YOU'RE HAVING FUN.

As busy mamas, any sort of down time we can find is scarce at best. We are girls with some hefty responsibilities who often struggle to find enough hours in the day to achieve what we need to get done. We're used to arguments in the car, sibling scuffles at home, and the rambunctious chaos that comes along with having young children. We're *not* accustomed to peace and quiet, nor are we familiar with what to do with ourselves once we get it. Free time often finds us torn between achieving some type of productivity by running some much-needed errands for the family, or pursuing something solely for ourselves—an area where some of us Super Moms tend to struggle. You see, rather than embracing the moments we have all by our lonesome, oftentimes we're bombarded with feelings of guilt, instead. *How can I possibly take a break? Won't my children think I'm abandoning them? How will my family function without me?*

Believe me, girls . . . I understand.

Once that proverbial switch of motherhood has been flipped on, there is indeed no way of turning it off. Our minds often wander toward worry when our children aren't underfoot or in our possession. Our thoughts and lives have been and will continue to be consumed by those amazing kiddos we've been given; but it doesn't change the fact that no matter how dedicated we may be, every mommy is in need of a break from time to time. So, ditch the guilt, cast aside all of that worrying, and let's take the opportunity to refresh our minds, bodies, and most importantly, our spirits. May I remind you that even God—the Almighty—rested after six long days of hard work (Gen. 2:2), so even though we may not have created the world or the vast number of species within it, we are the appointed caretakers of God's most precious creatures. And that, my friends, requires a break every now and then.

Don't you agree? I thought so.

Oh, and PS: whether you choose to accept this advice or not, I must voice my opinion by stating that our "earned free time" should be about us . . . not the pesky busy-work comprised of replenishing our pantries or crossing off one more errand on those unending to-do lists. Nope, the few hours of time you've got is all about spending time on Y-O-U! It's time for mama to relax, recharge, renew . . . and have a little fun, too. So, let's take a minute to explore just some of the joy to be had while flying solo and taking a much-deserved mini-hiatus.

**Go to lunch.** We're not talking about peanut butter and jelly sandwiches. We're talking about sitting down—at a restaurant other than IHOP and perhaps with a best girlfriend or two—and indulging in a meal that has not been prepared, cooked, or served by *you*. A luncheon that will require absolutely no effort on your part. No cleaning up drinks spilt by your little ones, no crumbs of food all over the floor, and no dissecting food to make sure the pieces aren't too large for the younger ones to gnaw on. This lunch is all about enjoying adult-time together, with food you can actually take the time to delight in. Bon appetit!

**Read a book.** Yes. As in an actual book, like the one in your hands. Catch up on the latest in a popular series or national bestseller. Or, take the time to freshen up on current events and world news by reading a newspaper, your favorite columnist, or by leisurely reading a magazine. Plop down in an oversized chair at your favorite bookstore and immerse yourself in another world, even if it is only for a few hours. Who cares what you're reading. If it's what you desire to do, then by all means, go for it . . . interruption free, that is. *Woot, woot!*

**Pamper yourself.** Hellooooo day spa! Now, I don't care what you say here, every girl is in need of a little pampering from time to time. Whether it's a pedicure, a massage, a facial, or even something as simple as getting your hair done, we ladies need (and deserve) some good old rest and relaxation. So call ahead, make an appointment, and let someone else tend to your needs for a little while. It may be just what you need.

**Take a class.** Okay, just hear me out on this one because you're probably wondering why I would recommend adding more work to your already chaotic schedule. But think about this for a minute: many of us moms love to tap into our creative side, right? We might like entertaining our left-brain by enjoying hobbies such as scrapbooking, photography, art, sewing, or anything else that sparks our interest and imagination. If this sounds like you, then what are you waiting for? Embrace your free time by signing up for a course that will indulge the artistic side that's been begging to get out. Check out classes offered in your area and take pleasure in your own personal pastime.

**Catch a flick.** How often do we get the opportunity to see a movie *we'd* like to watch, ladies? I'll admit that I am a people-pleaser of sorts, which means that ever since meeting and marrying my husband, my outings to chick flicks have been few and very far between. By the time my man and I finally decide upon a movie as part of our date night activity, we usually end up choosing an action-packed feature film, rather than the hilarious girl comedy I'd prefer. Sometimes, I just want to take pleasure in a humor-filled film that only gals like us can understand. I want to LOL, all while enjoying a big old tub of buttery popcorn, a box of Milk Duds perhaps, and one bladder-busting carbonated beverage to wash it all down with. Who else is with me? Well, if you've got free time, check your local listings and make a date with yourself to do just that.

**Work it out.** A workout is a great way to release some endorphins and reduce some of that pent-up stress that may have been building over the past week, month, or year. Take a jog, go for a bike ride around the neighborhood, or partake in an aerobics class at the gym (especially if you indulged in the tasty activities I mentioned above). Whatever you like to do in order to get your sweat on, just do it! Exercise can be great for the soul and an excellent stress-reliever that can do a body some serious good. As Olivia Newton-John always said, "Let's get physical!"

**Get retail relief**. Admittedly, this is where I tend to spend most of my free time. Some of you may be able to relate, but for others this may be the last place on earth you'd want to waste any of your time, let alone those rare, kiddie-free moments we're discussing. I, for one, take pleasure in finding deals on new duds to wear without having to listen to my children complain of boredom, or without having to start a mall-wide search party because they've wandered off without my realizing it. I also like to be methodical in my purchases by experiencing a few moments of uninterrupted thought in order to figure out what I'm buying, how much I'm spending, and if I *really* need this garment or not. So, if you find retailing therapeutic, then grab your purse, your department store coupons, set your budget, and get to shoppin' . . . solo style!

**Have a snooze fest.** Sometimes, catching up on some much-needed rest is the perfect way to spend some downtime. Just writing about it has me wanting to jump into my coziest pair of pajamas and head off to bed for a long winter snooze. If you find yourself in the category of needing some extra Zs, consult your husband (or family member) about taking the kiddos out of the house for a bit. Just three hours of slumber can do a world of wonder for a mom suffering from sleep deprivation.

**Be productive**. Yes, you read this right . . . but not because I'm recommending it. Remember—I feel that any downtime you receive should be spent on you, not the errands you have to do. But after polling my mommy friends on Facebook, the number one activity most of them wanted to achieve during moments of pure solitude involved checking off items on their to-do lists. Now, I can understand that by doing so, you're able to get more done than, say, if your children were present. I can also see where this can in fact reduce levels of stress as well, but these types of activities certainly won't leave us refreshed, now will they? Productive? Yes! Renewed in mind, body, and spirit? Ummm, no! Plain and simple, ladies: make time for yourselves, partake in activities you enjoy doing, and resist the urge to place yourself last while putting those unending tasks first.

**Pray.** If we've got quiet time to ourselves, sounds like the perfect atmosphere to foster a chat with God. So, sit down with your Bible, bring out the devotional, and spend some moments deep in prayer. Pray for your children, their protection, their health, and their future. Pray for your husbands (or perhaps future husbands), for his leadership, partnership, and understanding, and for his center to be in Christ. Pray for strength, wisdom, patience, and clarity in your role as your children's mother. Call on God to meet you where you need Him the most. Invest in your future by spending time with Him in the present. You'll be glad you did.

## AVOIDING B-U-R-N-O-U-T

As we've already mentioned, Wonder Woman Wannabes need some time to ourselves every now and then. And as you've probably already experienced, it's no surprise that when we don't receive our "breaks," burnout and subsequent mommy meltdowns are bound to occur. Yikes! These are the types of episodes we'd like to avoid because they disregard any effort we make to embody the patient, loving, doting, and relaxed mothers we so desire to be. Needless to say, making the commitment to engage in free time is a necessity, just as making space on our calendars to do so needs to become mandatory. Let's avoid these burnouts before they occur, girls, by taking a few precautionary steps to do just that.

*The Mad Hatter: "Have I gone mad?"*
*Alice: "I'm afraid so. You're entirely bonkers.*
*But I'll tell you a secret. All the best people are."*

**—Alice in Wonderland (film version directed by Tim Burton)**

**Make a plan.** Schedule at least two times per month, if not more, where dad, grandparents, or a sitter can watch the kids while you step out on your own. Warning: this does not include date night with your spouse, either. This is independent time just for you and no one else. Make a plan, schedule it on the calendar, and execute as often as needed. Oh, and remember to enjoy yourself, too!

**Stick to a budget.** "Mommy Times" are necessary for us girls in order to save our sanity, but so is sticking to a budget. Plan your days ahead and save up if need be. Look for deals locally, bring coupons as often as possible, and search for activities that won't deplete your bank funds to mere pennies. Establish and stick to a budget that both you and your spouse can agree on together. *Cha-ching!*

**No cancellations.** You've made a promise to yourself to take more breaks and get more rest as you attempt to ease the tensions and subsequent stress that can accompany this role of being a mommy. If you've made this vow to yourself, then by all means, you've got to stick to it. Basically, no cancellations allowed, girls! After all, it is only two days a month, and that's certainly not a lot to ask for ourselves—let alone feel guilty about. Side note: summertime schedules may need to be altered and upgraded depending on offspring's behavior.

We are all likely to reach burnout mode if we aren't taking the necessary steps to avoid it. When you think about it—I mean really think about it—you went from being a girl with all the time in the world to a woman with some pretty major responsibilities and practically no time to herself. You need and deserve these breaks, and you can't neglect giving your mind and body the time it needs to relax and reboot.

*Ommmm.* See . . . relaxed already. Now, make a date with yourself and stick to it.

Relax, recharge, and get re-energized!

# 19

# WAVING THE WHITE FLAG—THE WANNABE SURRENDERS

*"Imagine all the wondrous things your arms might embrace if they weren't wrapped so tightly around your struggles."*

**—Sheila Burke**

*My Dear Wonder Woman Wannabe (the younger, less wrinkly version of myself that is):*

*As I think back upon days gone by—you know, the ones you're experiencing right now—I wish I could tell you that it'll get easier. I wish I could say that the worries you're experiencing will subside, your stress will totally diminish, and that those all-too-familiar struggles you're presently battling will waste away altogether. But I'd be lying if I did.*

*You see, precious mama, as I sit here writing this letter to you—my younger self—I'm painfully reminded of all of that frustration, not to mention exhaustion, we endured while raising our young brood. In fact, I'm getting tired just thinking about it—no really, I'm old and napping is my pastime. It's what I "do" these days. But I'll tell you what: as hard as those times in the trenches of young motherhood were, I have to confess that now more than ever, I miss them. As ridiculous as this may sound, I long for the hectic lifestyle, the crazy schedule we kept, and I even miss those monotonous carpools in the minivan, too. I'd do anything to be able to have some of those moments back, and to be able to snuggle up with those babies of ours once again. Gosh, sometimes you just don't realize the blessings you have until they're gone . . . or grown-up that is.*

*Wait. Are you rolling your eyes? I know, I know—we used to despise when those sentiments were flung our way by other women in the midst of our mommy madness, but whether you're tired of hearing these words or not (and as much as I hate to admit them), time flies, girl . . . faster than I ever thought possible.*

*So, wake up, and enjoy those little monsters of yours while they're still young, and before they get too much older. Stop trying to control your life and understand that the pilot's seat of your adventure is already occupied by the One who created you. Don't fret over the laundry or the list of chores in need of your attention—even though I know how much they annoy you and cause your OCD to go a little wonky. Just take the time to appreciate that those children, whom you helped bring into this world, want nothing more than to spend time with their totally fun, super hip (and completely unstressed) mama. They want you, girl, not the perfectionist you're hoping to be . . . and especially not that Wonder Woman character you're choosing to chase after (psst: they don't even know who she is).*

*Are you listening? Just be you! Be goofy and silly, and enjoy those memorable mommy-moments you were meant to have—yes, even the ones where the little one screams his head off and runs around the house naked. Because one day, you'll become this old lady, sitting here, writing this letter with only the memories you took the time to make.*

*Remember, God isn't calling you to be perfect. And why would He, anyway? His intention was never to clone Himself; rather, His calling for you is to mother your kiddos to the best of your abilities. His desire for you is to adore your children (His children) by becoming the superhero in their eyes, not your own.*

*So get out your white flag, and resign from those perfectionist ways once and for all. Believe me—you'll be so glad you did.*

*Love,*
*Your older—less mobile, but full of wisdom—self,*
*Jenny*

## GET OUT THOSE WHITE FLAGS, GIRLS.

Wow, we've certainly been through a lot together throughout this book, haven't we? Gosh, I've probably told you more about myself in these here pages than any of you would've ever cared to know in the first place. But when it comes to raising kids and helping one another out in the process, too much information can be a good thing. A really good thing, in fact. But in all seriousness, my prayer throughout this book has been that each of you could identify yourself within these pages . . . because as women, we may have a number of differences, but as mothers, we share too many similarities to count. Just like me, you may be facing trials, mayhem, and daily battles of your own. Just like me, you might be in need of some assistance, guidance, and/or a friend who can relate to and understand your dilemma(s). Girls, I pray that this guide and the advice it contains have given you just that: a friend to relate to, and a sister in the trenches.

But there's something else I'd like to bring to your attention.

You see, no matter how many tips we glean, nor how efficient, organized, or task-oriented we become in our roles as mothers, it can't hide the fact that we'll never become perfect. No matter how hard we try or how much time we waste in securing such a title . . . it's simply impossible. And no matter how full our plates become or how often we strive to stay on top of it all and whether we succeed, fail, or mess the entire thing up completely, God will be there for us, dishing out huge helpings of grace, along with some major doses of mercy. And all we ladies have to do is make the choice to embrace it.

So what do you say we bust out that white flag? What do you think? Surrender, give up, and finally scream, "Uncle?" I mean, isn't it time we resign from our plights with perfectionism once and for all—isn't it time to stand tall, and willingly ditch all of our failures with flawlessness for some much-needed, God-given grace instead?

*"For it is by grace you have been saved, through faith— and this not from yourselves, it is the gift of God— not by works so that no one can boast."*

**—Ephesians 2:8–9**

But hold on just a second. Before we officially stake our claim, I must make mention of one more thing. You see, right now might also be the time when we choose to redefine what this Wonder Woman gal is all about. By shattering her stereotypes and debunking the myths surrounding her, we can better grasp what being a *real* woman of wonder is all about.

Are you ready?

I mean, *really* ready?

Yah. Me, too.

## RECLAIMING WONDER WOMAN

> *"God sees in you a masterpiece about to happen."*
>
> **—Max Lucado**

Now as I think back upon those days as a kid, you know—the times I spent running around, Underoo-clad, and pretending to be a heroine of some sort—I never would have imagined that the very superwoman I hoped to embody would one day be the gal holding me hostage in my unrealistic expectations and lame desires for perfection. Those star-spangled bloomers, that red corset, and that shiny gold crown/cuff combination had me tricked into believing something that just wasn't real, as I spent most of my young adult life struggling to become "super" in one way or another.

I hate when I learn stuff the hard way!

But, throughout my years as a mom, I've managed to realize a few things. Our lives, and the sole purpose in living them, should in no way, shape, or form be about rising to the impossible standards society has set for us. As a mother, my identity doesn't reside in meaningless things, nor do I want it to. I don't want to be considered super because I mop a mean floor, dust the dickens out of my furniture, or whip up a magically delicious meatloaf on the fly. Instead, I want to be deemed wondrous because I choose to follow a God who tells me so. One who created me—*me!*—in His very image, who sent a Savior to free me from my sins, and who has a plan in mind that not even I can wrap my head around. God considers me to be a wondrous woman already, and loves me just the way I am . . . imperfections and all.

Girls, maybe we should consider ourselves to be Wonder Woman Wannabes because we're striving to *become* the women *God* intended us to be. Maybe our roles as mothers should have everything do with following Him and His desires, and less to do with us. Maybe, just maybe here, we should attempt to take the focus off of ourselves . . . and place it on *Him*, instead.

Essentially, let's reclaim what Wonder Woman is all about.

And let's start by mothering our children to the best of our abilities and loving them unconditionally. Let's choose to forget about comparisons and competition. And those mounting pressures we've placed upon ourselves? We can get rid of those, too. Let us assume our places and fulfill the roles God designed each of us to embody . . . and let's equip ourselves to do so.

> *"Finally, be strong in the Lord and in his mighty power. Put on the full armor of God, so that you can take your stand against the devil's schemes. For our struggle is not against flesh and blood, but against the rulers, against the authorities, against the powers of this dark world and against the spiritual forces of evil in the heavenly realms."*
>
> **—Ephesians 6:10–12**

So, go ahead moms, and begin each one of your days by staking your claim as a real Wonder Woman. Position that tiara high upon your head—as a reminder that you are a daughter of the King. Get on those gold cuffs and deflect the negativity, frustration, and exhaustion that are attempting to attack from all angles. Take that lasso of truth and keep it close by as a symbol that the Evil One will stop at nothing to trick you into believing the lies of this world. Don that corset—well, maybe a more modest version, that is—and shield your hearts from the hurt, doubts, fear, shame, and guilt that moms like us are plagued with at one time or another. And finally, put on that pair of stiletto boots (the higher the heel, the better), and use them to willingly stomp out the enemy, the comparisons, the competition, the pressures, and the killjoys of motherhood.

Wave that white flag, embrace your Wannabe status, ditch those desires for all things perfect, put your game face on, and meet God in the midst of it all. Let's vow to do our best, and allow Him—you know, the One who created the world and civilization itself—to take care of the details for us from here on out.

Hey, we may not have been born an Amazon Princess, but we are the daughters of the King, and it's about time we start realizing it.

It's time to let go, girls . . . and it's time to let God.

*"Trust in the Lord with all your heart,*
*and do not lean on your own understanding.*
*In all your ways acknowledge him,*
*and he will make straight your paths."*

**—Proverbs 3:5–6 ESV**